Political Decision–Making and Security Intelligence:

Recent Techniques and Technological Developments

Luisa Dall'Acqua
University of Bologna, Italy & LS TCO, Italy

Irene M. Gironacci
Swinburne University of Technology, Australia

A volume in the Advances in
Electronic Government, Digital
Divide, and Regional Development
(AEGDDRD) Book Series

Published in the United States of America by
    IGI Global
    Information Science Reference (an imprint of IGI Global)
    701 E. Chocolate Avenue
    Hershey PA, USA 17033
    Tel: 717-533-8845
    Fax: 717-533-8661
    E-mail: cust@igi-global.com
    Web site: http://www.igi-global.com

Library of Congress Cataloging-in-Publication Data

Names: Dall'Acqua, Luisa, 1962- author. | Gironacci, Irene M., 1988- author.
Title: Political decision-making and security intelligence : recent techniques and technological developments / by Luisa Dall'Acqua and Irene M. Gironacci.
Description: Hershey, PA : Information Science Reference, 2020. | Includes bibliographical references and index. | Summary: """This book examines the main techniques of intelligence analysis to prevent terrorism and political attacks conducted by state/non-state actors. It also explores the use of new technologies as investigative tools and training"--Provided by publisher"-- Provided by publisher.
Identifiers: LCCN 2019031676 (print) | LCCN 2019031677 (ebook) | ISBN 9781799815624 (h/c) | ISBN 9781799815716 (s/c) | ISBN 9781799815631 (ebook)
Subjects: LCSH: Intelligence service--Technological innovations. | Intelligence service--Methodology. | Terrorism--Prevention. | National security--Decision making.
Classification: LCC JF1525.I6 D35 2020 (print) | LCC JF1525.I6 (ebook) | DDC 327.12--dc23
LC record available at https://lccn.loc.gov/2019031676
LC ebook record available at https://lccn.loc.gov/2019031677

This book is published in the IGI Global book series Advances in Electronic Government, Digital Divide, and Regional Development (AEGDDRD) (ISSN: 2326-9103; eISSN: 2326-9111)

British Cataloguing in Publication Data
A Cataloguing in Publication record for this book is available from the British Library.

All work contributed to this book is new, previously-unpublished material.
The views expressed in this book are those of the authors, but not necessarily of the publisher.

For electronic access to this publication, please contact: eresources@igi-global.com.

Advances in Electronic Government, Digital Divide, and Regional Development (AEGDDRD) Book Series

ISSN:2326-9103
EISSN:2326-9111

Editor-in-Chief: Zaigham Mahmood, University of Derby, UK & North West University, South Africa

MISSION

The successful use of digital technologies (including social media and mobile technologies) to provide public services and foster economic development has become an objective for governments around the world. The development towards electronic government (or e-government) not only affects the efficiency and effectiveness of public services, but also has the potential to transform the nature of government interactions with its citizens. Current research and practice on the adoption of electronic/digital government and the implementation in organizations around the world aims to emphasize the extensiveness of this growing field.

The **Advances in Electronic Government, Digital Divide & Regional Development (AEGDDRD)** book series aims to publish authored, edited and case books encompassing the current and innovative research and practice discussing all aspects of electronic government development, implementation and adoption as well the effective use of the emerging technologies (including social media and mobile technologies) for a more effective electronic governance (or e-governance).

COVERAGE

- E-Citizenship, Inclusive Government, Connected Government
- Knowledge Divide, Digital Divide
- Public Information Management, Regional Planning, Rural Development
- Social Media, Web 2.0, and Mobile Technologies in E-Government
- Issues and Challenges in E-Government Adoption
- Case Studies and Practical Approaches to E-Government and E-Governance
- ICT Infrastructure and Adoption for E-Government Provision
- Emerging Technologies within the Public Sector
- Electronic Government, Digital Democracy, Digital Government
- Citizens Participation and Adoption of E-Government Provision

IGI Global is currently accepting manuscripts for publication within this series. To submit a proposal for a volume in this series, please contact our Acquisition Editors at Acquisitions@igi-global.com or visit: http://www.igi-global.com/publish/.

Titles in this Series

For a list of additional titles in this series, please visit:
https://www.igi-global.com/book-series/advances-electronic-government-digital-divide/37153

Cases on Electronic Record Management in the ESARBCA Region
Segomotso Masegonyana Keakopa (University of Botswana, Botswana) and Tshepho Lydia
Mosweu (University of Botswana, Botswana)
Information Science Reference • © 2020 • 300pp • H/C (ISBN: 9781799825272) • US
$195.00

*Digital Transformation and Its Role in Progressing the Relationship Between States and
Their Citizens*
Sam B. Edwards III (Quinnipiac University, USA) and Diogo Santos (Pitágoras College,
Brazil & Estácio de Sa University, Brazil)
Information Science Reference • © 2020 • 300pp • H/C (ISBN: 9781799831525) • US
$185.00

Employing Recent Technologies for Improved Digital Governance
Vasaki Ponnusamy (Universiti Tunku Abdul Rahman, Malaysia) Khalid Rafique (Azad
Jammu and Kashmir Information Technology Board, Pakistan) and Noor Zaman (Taylor's
University, Malaysia)
Information Science Reference • © 2020 • 383pp • H/C (ISBN: 9781799818519) • US
$195.00

Tools, Strategies, and Practices for Modern and Accountable Public Sector Management
Graça Azevedo (University of Aveiro, Portugal) Jonas Oliveira (Instituto Universitário de
Lisboa (ISCTE-IUL), Portugal) Rui Pedro Marques (University of Aveiro, Portugal) and
Augusta Ferreira (University of Aveiro, Portugal)
Information Science Reference • © 2020 • 372pp • H/C (ISBN: 9781799813859) • US
$215.00

Examining the Roles of IT and Social Media in Democratic Development and Social Change
Vikas Kumar (Chaudhary Bansi Lal University, India) and Geetika Malhotra (Chaudhary
Bansi Lal University, India)
Information Science Reference • © 2020 • 384pp • H/C (ISBN: 9781799817918) • US
$195.00

701 East Chocolate Avenue, Hershey, PA 17033, USA
Tel: 717-533-8845 x100 • Fax: 717-533-8661
E-Mail: cust@igi-global.com • www.igi-global.com

Table of Contents

Preface... vii

Acknowledgment xvii

Section 1
Techniques of Analysis

Chapter 1
Policymakers and Intelligence Analysts as Decision-Making Agents...................1

Chapter 2
Policy-Decision Environment and Cognitive Biases: Cases Study.....................40

Chapter 3
Policy Making, Crisis Management, and Leadership Intelligence: A New
Framework of Analysis 61

Chapter 4
Intelligence Analysis, Uncertainty, and Risk Analysis 79

Chapter 5
Measures of Success for Intelligence Analysis and Products 92

Section 2
Technologies of Support

Chapter 6
Intelligence Analysis Sources: From HUMINT to TECHINT 106

Chapter 7
Cyber Intelligence and Security: State of the Art...123

Chapter 8
Using Extended Reality to Support Cyber Security 146

About the Authors.. 167

Index.. 168

Preface

To date, research on both human and machine intelligence has been characterized by a diversity of theoretical perspectives, empirical approaches, and applications. A defining characteristic of the Science of Intelligence is the synthetic approach to research. This approach requires that each insight, method, concept, and theory must demonstrate its merit by contributing to the generation of intelligent behavior in a synthetic artifact, such as a robot, or an intelligence investigation.

There is a multitude of intelligence-related disciplines. The main five categories are those concerned with creating embodied agents, those that study computational aspects of intelligence, those that are concerned with natural intelligence, those that study the biological substrates of intelligence, and those that study the intelligence investigation in the decision-making process.

Scientific Intelligence offers an innovative path of analysis of information deriving from different fields of knowledge (scientific, technological, behavioral, legal and investigative), multifactorial responses to the different needs in the field of risk management, safety, investigations and applied intelligence.

The specific sector of application of this research is the Security Intelligence and political decision-making, and the book aims to provide a theoretical foundation and empirical support for analyzing the development of a range of techniques and useful technologies in the sector. Policymakers require action analysis or intelligence deliverables which empowers them in successfully carrying out their role, in many and new sectors of investigations.

This book proposes transdisciplinary research, enabling progress towards a complete understanding of intelligence analysis. The proposed Science of Intelligence aims to establish intelligence research as a unified scientific discipline.

The research immerses the reader in contemporary trends and emerging paradigms within safety and security at both local and global levels and explores some justifications for the increasing 'securitization' of social life. It explores how Intelligence studies as an original path that represents a synthesis of humanistic and scientific disciplines, to identify a professional profile highly requested by the market. The acquired knowledge has interdisciplinary multi-applications. The contribution of the disciplines involved, alongside the various diagnostic tools in investigative, legal, operational, tactical, technological and psychological-behavioral fields, allow users to respond holistically to new and fluid needs.

The Authors examine the main techniques of Intelligence Analysis to prevent terrorism and political attacks conducted by state/non-state actors, and the use of new technologies as investigative tools and training for practitioners. The manuscript clearly demonstrates the power and utility of academic intersectionality between Intelligence science and practice.

Security Studies addresses a number of fundamental issues, the most important of which is what means the concept "Security Intelligence". Some scholars retain that the discipline focus is purely on military conflict and there are those who argue that in a globalized world Security Studies needs to be expanded to a consideration of economic, environmental as well as social issues

In 2008, NATO formulated new scenarios, in terms of security, through the new Strategic Concept - defining cyberterrorism as an attack of an IT nature that uses the network or sufficient communications to generate destruction or interruption, to create fear or to intimidate the members of a society into an ideological goal in the political and legal sphere; however the concept of security is not uniquely defined in all the nations of the planet.

With the attack on the Twin Towers, international terrorism and cyber-terrorism showed the radical change they had been subjected to, consequently forcing the super-powers' security apparatuses to modify their organizational and operational assets.

As said terrorist organizations have undergone a change over the last few years, it is enough to see Al Qaeda that has gone through three phases, each of which characterized by a particular configuration.

Initially, the organization was based on a central operational directive flanked by a large base of cells, then by a structure called chain network; subsequently, in the second phase, we moved on to a star-network model in which the central board had gained more grip on the territory and began to enjoy the support of delocalized cells.

Finally, in the third and final phase, with the full-matrix network model, the summit has become an ideological-media pole immersed in an extensive virtual network in addition to a number of dormant cells located internationally.

The diffusion of new technologies, especially communication and information technologies, continues at ever faster rates than the diffusion rates of previous technologies. This is mainly due to a change in globalization and greater economic, financial and productive integration of the digital society.

New technologies are becoming increasingly socially pervasive, replacing human presence in many sectors. Technological evolution changed people and the world. It means both risk and opportunities. An example of a use of technology is in the medical field: doctors can operate from different parts of the world through an internet connection. The same happens with the self-driving airplanes or the promotion of nurse-robots that will help people. But possible security threats can cause huge damages.

Specifically, the dissemination of these tools has both political and social implications. The effects of global events and transformations on foreign policy, such as the increase in the technology of nuclear weapons and chemical warfare, or how global communication sites during the Arab Spring, change the caution of policy-makers, pushing to empower global pacts and enter into more international organizations using platforms such as the UN.

The enormous spread of devices, for example, gives access to virtual networks and to cyberspace areas, where continuous flows of data and information are exchanged, increasing the risk of:

- Information warfare: dissemination and acquisition of data in order to obtain military and political information superiority on certain strategic objectives
- cyber-espionage: conducted for the purpose of violating intellectual property and patents of governments and companies
- cybercrime: often economic, with the aim of creating financial damage to businesses or economic actors
- cracking of virtual products on the net
- identity hacking, information systems and functions

The protection of personal data and intellectual property has become a priority for many governments. The number of individuals and companies that suffer data breaches has increased vertically, with serious reputational and economic damage internationally. Cyber hacking is becoming a real "business model", using attacks as services, creating fake videos to spread fake news. The risk also increases due to sensitive data concerning national, political and governmental security (Antinori, 2011).

The changes inherent to the new technologies by terrorist organizations have concerning the use of the Internet for the execution or preparation of the attack, as well as for the strengthening of the organization itself. The network is used, in fact, as a weapon when the attack has the objective of damaging or invalidating the computer systems or infrastructures of a given country, while it can be used as a means to find information, know-how, proselytes, funds of financing and substances useful to the terrorist action, previously difficult and differently available (Lamberti, 2014).

The location of the various cells in every part of the world, linked each other, has allowed the realization of the main attacks in the Western world, facilitating the planning of attacks and the preparation of terrorists. Also, the attacks in the Madrid and London metros (in 2004 and 2005 respectively) were carried out by cells, which, in this case, were only indirectly connected to the core of the organization. They have however been attributed to Al Qaeda, both for the numerous claims by the terrorist group, and because the modalities and the ends of the action have demonstrated the link between the Qaedist movements and the heart of the organization.

In 2010, Al-Qaeda founded an online magazine to spread the Qaedist message beyond the borders of the Muslim world, Inspire, which has become not only the main propaganda tool, but also and above all the source from which to find technical information / strategic for the preparation of the attacks, as happened for the Boston marathon attack in which it was discovered that the bombs had been built with pressure cookers full of explosives, nails and ball bearings; and for the Madrid and London, for which the Internet was the source from which to draw inspiration and technical information for the creation of explosives.

The phenomenon of Cyberterrorism is becoming more and more dangerous. In fact it is economic, anonymous, it can be carried out at a distance, it has an impressive amount of objectives at its disposal, it makes recruitment easy and fundraising, it can strike, though not always lethally, an extremely large number of objectives and, finally, it is capable of generating much greater coverage on the part of the media, a goal particularly sought after by terrorists.

In Europe, the first historical prevention plan in the field of cybercrime was issued in 1989 by the Director of Criminal Problems Committee (CDPC) of the Council of Europe in the form of Recommendation No. 9/89 on crime. This Recommendation has as a starting point the analysis of a double typology of cybercrime, on the basis of which, to example, Italy issued

Law 547/93. In it, fact, 1) the criminal conduct is described that European states must pursue criminally, as Italy did, and 2) a series of less serious and behaviors are indicated, less prejudicial than those contained in the other list, for which however a law enforcement action by the national legislator was nevertheless appropriate. Within this last list, by way of example, the conduct of unauthorized alteration of data or programs (in the absence of damage), or disclosure of information related to industrial or commercial secrecy (cases attributable to IT espionage) was indicated and unauthorized use of a computer or a protected computer program.

A second Recommendation No. 13 in 1995 concerned the procedures to be followed at various levels in cases of crimes committed in the Information Technology (IT) context. It expressed the relative concern, on the one hand, to the risk that electronic information systems can be used to commit crimes and, from the other to the failure to provide, within the legal systems of the Member States, appropriate powers such as to encourage the collection of evidence during investigations. On this last aspect, in particular, the Recommendation affirms the importance of the adoption of a regulatory apparatus that allows investigative authorities to make use of all the technical measures necessary to allow the collection of data traffic in the investigation of serious offenses to the confidentiality, integrity, and security of telematic and IT communications.

In 1997, the Council of Europe (CoE) formed a Committee of Experts on Crime in Cyber-space, and met in secret for several years drafting an international treaty entitled the "Convention on Cybercrime," (the Convention) that was released in final form in June (CECC, 2019). It included the task of drafting an international convention to combat and repress the crime within the information space, in order to facilitate international cooperation in investigations and effective persecution of computer-crimes by Member States.

Only in 2001, the Convention on Cybercrime (CC, 2001) was launched in Budapest, which provides for the adoption, at a national level, of regulatory measures that allow the development of a common policy aimed at protecting various States from computer crimes, as well as greater international cooperation.

In view of the described panorama, the Commission therefore identifies measures to be adopted with absolute priority and in particular:

- Awareness raising, that is, the launch of an information and public education campaign promoting the best practices in the sector;

- A European reporting and information system with consequent strengthening by the member states of their intervention agencies in case of IT emergency (CERT) and coordination of their activities;
- Technological support intended as support for research and development activities in the field of safety;
- Support for standardization and certification according to a market logic (the Commission invites the European standardization bodies to speed up work on the subject interoperability; furthermore, it reiterates the full support of the electronic signature and the development of the IPv6 and IPSec protocols; and furthermore, dwells its attention on the need for regulatory intervention on the subject of mutual recognition of certificates, with an invitation to member states to review their respective safety regulations);
- The regulatory intervention with the specification of the intention to draw up an inventory of national measures adopted in accordance with the relevant Community law, as well as the intention to present a legislative proposal on cyber crime;
- The strengthening of security in the public administration of the Member States related, in particular, to e-government (online administration) and e-procurement (online public procurement) activities; firm invitation to the States of the Union to use electronic signature technologies in the provision of services to the public, as well as the Commission's commitment to strengthen the security specifications of its information and communication systems;
- International cooperation, with the commitment of the Commission to intensify dialogue with international partners and bodies on a network and information security.

HOW THIS BOOK WORKS

The analysis consists of key issues, problems, trends, and particularly new ideas and innovation emerging Intelligence science. Furthermore, it investigates questions, explanations of terms and concepts in order to probe further thinking.

This comprehensive and timely publication aims to be an essential reference source, building on the available studies on developing 'instruments of analysis' to train managers, analysts, politicians, and researchers.

The book aims to explore perspectives and approaches to Intelligence analysis and performance. It also aims to combine theoretical underpinnings with practical relevance, in order to sensitize insights into training activities to manage uncertainty and risks in the decision-making process. It mains a collective resource with comprehensive knowledge in the development of managerial and intelligence analysis competency, including industries, academics (researchers, lecturers, and advanced students), professional institutions and Governative Departments, not last Defence Department.

This book consists of two section and eight chapters. The first section focuses on some crucial approaches to Intelligence Analysis and decision-making process; the second one focuses on new challenges and technologies to support this process.. A brief description of each chapters follows:

Section 1: Techniques of Analysis

Chapter 1: Policymakers and Intelligence Analysts as Decision-Making Agents

The chapter considers what intelligence and analysis mean. It deals with issues pertaining to law enforcement, government agencies and the private sector combating crime and the use of proactive intelligence.

The key questions presented include: What is the relationship between policymakers and Intelligence analysts as decision-maker? What is their application to security related issues of criminology and the domain of public protection. The chapter contains a possible laboratory for Intelligence practioners, to get awareness of theory through practical exercises.

Chapter 2: Policy Decision Environment and Cognitive Biases – Case Study

The chapter analyzes possible cognitive biases in the decision-making process, and explores some cases study in the Foreign Policy decision-making, distinguished in groupthink and polythink types. Groupthink, or group thought is the word used in the scientific literature to indicate a pathology of the system of thought exhibited by members of a social group. On the opposite, Polithink means a plurality of opinions and views that leads to; deep disagreements and a conflict among group members divergent and disjointed foreign policy decision-making process. The chapter dedicates a section to the analysis of cases study. Finally, the chapter contains a possible laboratory for Intelligence practioners, to get awareness of theory through practical exercises.

Chapter 3: Policy Making, Crisis Management, and Leadership Intelligence – A New Framework of Analysis

This chapter explores how Leadership Analysts can support policymakers by producing and delivering written and oral assessments of foreign leaders and key decision-makers. It analyzes the main leadership profiles and characteristics, applying a new framework of analysis, called Orientism Management (OM), that propose 10 different Knowledge Management types. Some case studies are referred and analyzed.

Chapter 4: Intelligence Analysis, Uncertainty, and Risk Analysis

The chapter analyzed the concept of threat vs risk, focusing on possible risks identification criteria and the main analytical approaches for the risk management. It applies the concepts to the Intelligence Analysis,

Chapter 5: Measures of Success for Intelligence Analysis and Products

The chapter proposes an evaluation of Intelligence sources, action and the main crucial issues about the relationship between policy-makers and analysts. I focuses on an application of cognitive biases in the intelligence analysis context, and on ethical issues in the intelligence activities such as politicization and secrecy issues.

Section 2: Technologies of Support

Chapter 6: Intelligence Sources – From HUMINT to TECHINT

This chapter explores Intelligence sources and their different sectors of applications. It describes how they avoid strategic unexpected threats, forces, events and developments that are capable of threatening a nation's existence, and provide long-term expertise and stability to political appointees ad decision-makers. Special focus is dedicated to how decision-makers constantly need tailored and timely intelligence that will provide background, context, information and warning, as well as an assessment of the risks, benefits and the likely outcomes.

Chapter 7: Cyber Intelligence and Security – State of the Art

The starting point of the chapter is that the benefits of the information age are numerous, but nascent threats like transnational cyber terrorism and information warfare exist alongside the positive aspects of globalization. It concludes exploring new emerging challenges. Some cases study are referred and analyzed.

Chapter 8: Using Extended Reality to Support Cyber Security

The chapter starts with the state-of-the-art of virtual and augmented reality and focuses on an overview on the available extended reality technologies in the context of cyber security. It is an excellent description of the challenges involved and a solution is proposed. The chapter ends with a discussion of the solution and the proposal of future developments.

Luisa Dall'acqua
University of Bologna, Italy & LS TCO, Italy

Irene M. Gironacci
Swinburn University of Technology, Australia

REFERENCES

Antinori, A. (2011). Terrorism, communication and media. Design of an experimental model of criminological analysis. In R. Seven (Ed.), *Criminology and Victimology: Methodologies and operational strategies. Minerva.*

CC. (2001). *Convenzione sulla criminalità informatica.* Retrieved in: https://www.coe.int/en/web/conventions/full-list/-/conventions/treaty/185

CECC. (2019). *The Council of Europe's Convention on Cybercrime.* Retrieved in: https://epic.org/privacy/intl/ccc.html

Lamberti, C. (2014). Gli strumenti di contrasto al terrorismo e al cyber-terrorismo nel contesto europeo. Rivista di Criminologia, Vittimologia e Sicurezza, 8(2).

Acknowledgment

We wish to acknowledge the very valuable help and encouragement we received from our colleagues and friends. A special thank is for the students of Luisa dall'Acqua at the University of Bologna (Italy), regarding their hard work to test laboratories and to review the proposed literature.

We wish to place on record our deep appreciation and thanks to Ms. Maria Rohde, IGI Global Assistant Development Editor for her support, cooperation and attention to detail to bring out the publication of this book in time.

Lastly, we wish to thank our families for the understanding and support in providing us with all the necessary facilities to enable us to complete our work and above all, we are immensely thankful to the Almighty.

Section 1
Techniques of Analysis

Chapter 1
Policymakers and Intelligence Analysts as Decision–Making Agents

ABSTRACT

Decision making is a process of choosing among alternative courses of action to attain a goal(s). Specifically, managerial decision-making is a complex task in today's political/business environment. Information analysis is gathered by an intelligence analyst, as someone who is primarily responsible for the analysis, processing, and distribution of strategic and tactical intelligence. The chapter explores the main approaches to both policy cycle and intelligence cycle to make decisions.

TOPICS FOR DISCUSSION

The following discussion points come from information in this chapter:

1. What is the relationship between policy-makers and Intelligence analysts as decision-maker?
2. What is their application to security-related issues of criminology and the domain of public protection.

DOI: 10.4018/978-1-7998-1562-4.ch001

INTRODUCTION

What's public policy? A few definitions:

- Policy-making is everything a government decides to do or not to do (Colebatch, 2006).
- Policy-making is a set of decisions and activities related to the solution of a collective problem, need or demand for public intervention (Dunn, 1994).
- Policy-making is a set of concatenated and coherent decisions, taken by one or more public (sometimes private) actors in order to resolve, in a targeted way, a problem defined politically as collective (Knoepfel et al., 2007).
- The decision-making is a political process. The problem solving, as an adaptive process, leads to the analysis to find a solution requiring to make decisions, and induces the policy-maker to assume specific behaviors and actions (Mayer 2014).

In common these and other definitions have that a policy decision is a process of choosing between multiple solutions to a collective problem.

The distinguishing features of the policy processes area progressive complexity, the increase in uncertainty, and a possible increase in conflict. The wide array of features of the policy-making can influence policy decisions. The often-changing policy conditions taken into account identifying problems and deciding how to address them, such as:

- a political system's geography
- biophysical and demographic profile
- economy
- mass attitudes and behavior
- pre-existing laws, rules, institutions, and programs
- international political (and business) games

State secrecy, military secrecy, investigative secrecy, office secrecy, banking secrecy, industrial secrecy, are only a part of the institutional obstacles set on the government road of free information, and therefore of the knowledge of public affairs (C. Arcuri, 1990).

The politician does not have the time or inclination to absorb a vast amount of information. Knowledge is the true basis of national power and represents

Figure 1. Politicians and public decisions

the crucial element of the world struggle for the power of the futre. We need to produce an analysis capable of warning, illuminating and empowering politicians (Figure 1).

Policy Research

There are two types of policy research: research 'for' policy and research 'on' policy (Buse & Young, 2006). **Research 'for' policy** is about policy content (what should be done) and policy outcomes (policy evaluation). Research 'on' policy is about the policy process (usually not evaluative, focuses on 'how' and 'why' questions).

'**Research on policy** seeks to understand how the machinery of the state and political actors interact to produce public actions [...]. The main tasks [...] are to explain how policy-making works and to explore the variety and complexity of the decision-making processes.'

According to the basic Walt & Gilson's framework (see Figure 2) we can analyze the conen"the what" of a policy (content), those who affect and are affected by decisions (the actors), how decisions are made – the rules of the game (the process) and the social, cultural, temporal environment in which decisions taken (the context).

The constituent parts of the **content** sector are:

- aims and strategies of the policy
- underlying values and paradigms
- Administrative feasibility of the policy
- Empirical basis of the policy (evidence)
- Technical content (evidence informed)

3

Figure 2. Walt & Gilson's framework (Source: Walt & Gilson, 1994)

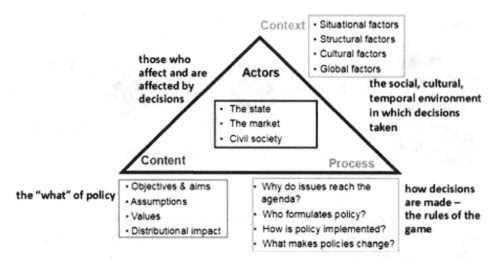

The constituent part of the **actors** sector is the distribution of benefits and costs in terms of Stakeholders, Scale, Characteristics, Intensity Timing. Specifically, Actors/Stakeholders are:

- Individuals or groups with interest in the issue:
  - Some role in making or implementing decision
  - Affected by policy decision
  - Specific to each policy reform and context
- Stakeholder analysis:
  - Identify stakeholder groups
  - Looking for independent groups/individuals with some influence or potential influence
  - Break down categories as far as feasible

Constituent variables of the **context** are:

- **Situational:** Change of leadership, focusing events, new evidence,.
- **Structural:** Resource allocation to intervention, organization of service delivery – public private mix
- **Cultural:** Prevailing attitudes to situation of women, technology, equity, tradition, etc.

- **International:** Place of intervention on international agenda, aid dependency, levels and modalities, migration of staff, ideas and paradigms, etc.

The constituent variable of the **process** sector is how the policy is initiated, developed, negotiated, communicated, implemented:

POLICY CYCLE

According to the traditional policy-analysis paradigm, decision maker is interested in the analysis of alternatives of actions to solve a problematic situation. The focus is on the evidence-informed policy challenging, a variety of tools to understand these factors, a range in sophistication/complexity and ease of use, Human / Technical Supports

The policy cycle is a way to organize relevant topics and an effective model of policy representation. It consists of 3macro-phases (see figure 3):

- Ex ante evaluation
  - *Agenda setting* (Problem finding*)*: acknowledgment of the problem
  - *Criteria* (Problem setting): the methodology to define the problem
  - *Analysis* (Problem analysis): break down the main problem into secondary problems
  - *Formulation and Design* (Problem solving proposal)
- In itinere evaluation
  - *Decision Making*: choice of the solution. It induces the decision-maker to assume specific behaviors and actions.
  - *Implementation*
- Ex post evaluation
  - *Final evaluation:* It is a results check.

Basically, the problem solving is a cognitive process with respect to a problem. Its goal is to achieve a goal. The problem discovered leads to the analysis to find a solution. The problem solving requires making decisions. It induces the subject to assume specific behaviors and actions. It is an adaptive process (Mayer 2014). Specifically, the goal of the formulation and design phase is to design a policy.

Figure 3. Policy Cycle and activities (freely adapted from https://debategraph.org/ Details.aspx?nid=228943)

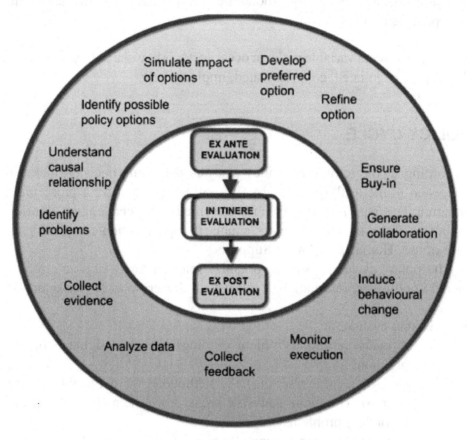

The first phase of the process concern of information gathering, scenario analysis and problem identification.

Data are raw and uninterpreted observations and measurements, such as computer - records, reports, statistics.

Information is data put into a context and empowered with a meaning, which gives it greater relevance and purpose, such as data in context, insights.

Knowledge is an information that has been given an interpretation and understanding, that is interpreted understood information.

Intelligence is data, information and knowledge that have been evaluated, analyzed and presented in a decision-making format for action-oriented purposes.

Figure 4. The relationship among the four Cardinal points

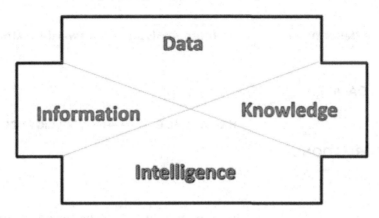

Analysis goes beyond the evidence of facts: It can tell you how good (or poor) your information/intelligence is. It can tell you things you didn't know before. It can tell you what you need to know to understand a situation. It

Figure 5. Analytical process

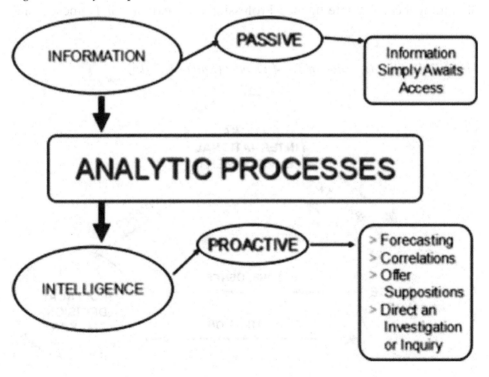

Figure 6. From description to analysis

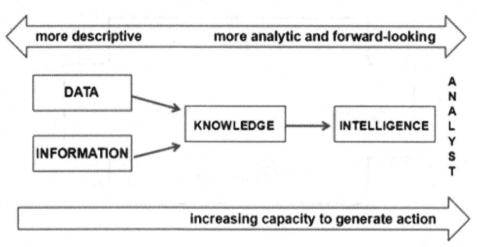

can tell you where to look further. It can help you to communicate your understanding to others.

All-source analysts are responsible for performing a more through evaluation and assessment of the collected information by integrating the data obtained from a variety of collection agencies and sources (Goldman, 2011). Words of Intelligence: An Intelligence Professional's Lexicon for Domestic and

Figure 7. Freely adaptation of The 4-i model (Ratcliffe, 2016)

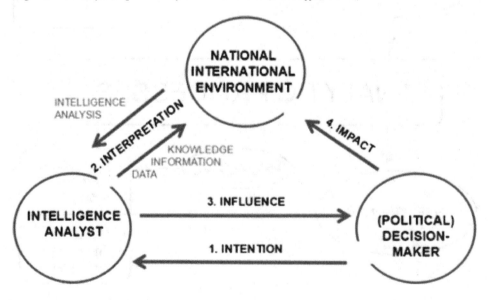

Figure 8. Influences on the policy maker analysis (Organization for Security and Co-Operation, 2017)

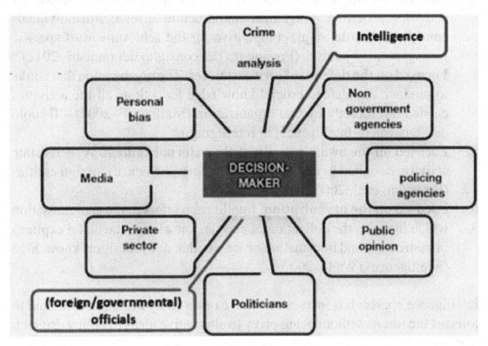

Foreign Threats, Security and Professional Intelligence Education Series, Scarecrow Press, UK).

A DEFINITIONS OF INTELLIGENCE

1. **Focused on the method.** It's the end product of an analytical process that:
    a.   evaluates information gathered from different sources
    b.   integrates the relevant information into a logical package
    c.   estimates and predicts actions
    d.   produces a conclusion of a phenomenon, using a scientific approach to problem-solving (analysis)
2. **Focused on action goals.** The value-added product resulting from the collection, evaluation, analysis, integration, interpretation of all available information regarding one or more aspects of a decision-making need (Fleisher, 2003):
    a.   to let decision-makers choose and adopt the better strategy

    b.   to decide in a timely, convenient and effective manner

3.   **Focused on the defence from a network of agents.** A complex of activities carried out by organizational structures in relation to individuals considered hostile, rival, competitive for the achievement of specific management objectives (Presidenza del consiglio dei ministri, 2012)

4.   **Focused on the defence of own resources.** The organization that works to produce and defend crucial knowledge for a State all the activities carried out secretly by that organization (Malfanti F. 2005). "Il ruolo dell'analista di Intelligence, in Intelligrate)

5.   **Focused on the awareness about the external context.** A secret state activity, designed to understand (sometimes influence) foreign entities (Reverton, et al.,2006)

6.   **Focused on the organization.** Intelligence refers to those organisation which includes the collection of people, knowledge (tacit and explicit) infrastructure and information processes that deliver critical knowledge (intelligence) (Waltz. 2003)

Intelligence approach is focused to reduce uncertainty of this analysis and to forecast the future without being privy to alternative ideas of policy decision makers.

Specifically, with the aim of protecting National Security, the word intelligence has a double meaning:

- **subjective**, which refers to the complex of structures and activities of an internal organization aimed at collecting useful information
- **objective**, which refers to the product of this activity (the information), functional to support the decision-making for the purposes of the protection of the national security

Policymakers require action analysis or intelligence deliverables which empowers them in successfully carrying out their unique role of establishing public policy.

Intelligence, as an ability to pre-empt and understand, will be the crux of the world struggle for the power of the future (Steele, 2000).

Intelligence Analysts are a task of experts in the field of analysis (politics, economics, technology, military, terrorism..) possesses knowledge, sufficient capacity for imagination and creativity to relate data, predict events. They are increasingly requested by the institutional apparatus responsible for national security and public security by companies, by public and private research centers, by the armed forces. Specifically:

- **Strategic intelligence** takes a "big picture" view of competitor/criminal/terrorist activity. It focuses on the long-term aims of law enforcement agencies, and, in a criminal context, on crime environment, threats to public safety and order, counter programmes, avenues for change to policies, programmes, and legislation.
- **Tactical intelligence** provides analysis, maps, and data to support an operation or disaster response effort, and fulfilling short term, case-specific needs
- **Operational intelligence** typically provides an investigative team with hypotheses and inferences concerning specific elements of illegal operations of any sort. These will include criminal networks, individuals or groups involved in unlawful activities, methods, capabilities, vulnerabilities, limitations and intentions

The "Secret" Agent

Secret Services are different from Political Bodies for targets, means and action method.

Police activities must be out in the open, acquire objective elements, have formal procedures, and have direct juridical effects to guarantee and restore the violated legal system.

Secret Services usually are in an occult manner, have flexible procedures and have not direct juridicial effects (*salus rei publicae*). They provide the political decision-maker with all the elements necessary for carrying out "special" operations abroad and into the national territory for the protection of national security, and repress the opponent's spacy. They can be:

- **Operational**: In the stage, activity of information acquisition.
- **Analyst**: In the office, information processing, interpretation and analysis.
- **Technician**: In the laboratory, specialized activity (translations, scientific analysis).

Table 1. Types of Intelligence Analysts

Type	Role
Detectives and Police agents	*who gather intelligence to study and solve crimes.Their targets range from organized crime, bank robberies, kidnapping, extortion and corruption, to civil rights violations and copyright infringements.*
Criminal Intelligence Analysts	use the qualitative and quantitative study of crime and police related information in combination with socio-demographic and spatial factors to apprehend criminals, prevent crime, reduce disorder, and evaluate organizational procedures
Tactical Crime Analysts	study recent criminal incidents and potential and possible criminal activity by examining characteristics such as how, when, and where the activity has occurred to assist in problem solving by developing patterns and trends, identifying investigative leads/suspects, and clearing cases.
Intelligence Research Specialists	work in a variety of areas to support domestic and international law enforcement agencies in combating money laundering and other financial crimes.
Civilian Intelligence Analysts	play a crucial role in supporting national security in a country. This analysts gather information from multiple sources (diplomatic reports, news wire services, media reports, specialist journals and sensitive intelligence materials) to prepare reports and briefings on international issues.
Counterintelligence Threat Analysts	examine reports related to foreign intelligence operations that threaten the governments or intelligence community
Counterterrorism Analysts	assess the leadership, plans, motivation and intentions of foreign terrorist groups to warn of terrorist threats
Crime and Counternarcotics Analysts	study emerging trends and patterns related to international narcotics trafficking and organized crime groups
Military Analysts	follow foreign military and technical developments that threaten regional or international stability
Leadership Analysts	examine information on foreign leaders and organizations for national policymakers
Business Intelligence (BI) Analyst	the BI Analyst is responsible for analyzing data and information that is used by a business or organization. Data used in BI generally supports decision-making. The BI analyst works with data to maximize the utility
Political Analysts	Examine foreign political, cultural, social, and historical information related to foreign political systems
Foreign Media Analysts	Examine foreign-based websites, social media and other press sources to identify trends and patterns
Medical and Health Analysts	Assess global health issues, such as disease outbreaks
Science and Technology Analysts	Examine weapons proliferation, conventional weapons systems, computer systems, etc.
Psychological and Psychiatric Analysts	Study the psychological and social health (for example of officials in charge or employees)
Targeting Analysts	*Identify key figures and organizations who may pose a threat to national or company interests using network analysis techniques and specialized analytical tools*

Intelligence Studies as an Academic Discipline

A debate currently exists about the respective roles and functions of intelligence analysis vs political decision-maker assessment.

In the 1950s, there was concern that the lack of literature on the intelligence profession. Ensuring that knowledge about the intelligence business would be captured and made accessible to others was uncertain (Marrin, 2016). Paucity has been resolved as both government and academies contributing literature to advance knowledge in the field.

Sherman Kent (1903-1986), father of Intelligence Analysis for the CIA, was the renowned Office of Strategic Services (OSS) and CIA intelligence analyst. He claimed that the "integrity" or independence of the analytic function had to be retained outside the direct line authority of the decision maker.

Willmoore Kendall (1909-1967), contemporary, was the defensor of the majority-rule democracy in America, a writer and the founder of the conservative movement. He disagreed with Kent, and believed that intelligence analysts should work in close cooperation with decisionmakers.He claimed that the "integrity" or independence of the analytic function had to be retained outside the direct line authority of the decision maker.

Roger Hilsman (1919-2014) was the 8th Assistant Secretary of State for Far Eastern Affairs and 2nd Director of the Bureau of Intelligence and Research. He argued, a more effective integration of knowledge and action—or intelligence analysis and decision making—will require intelligence analysts to become more policy-oriented.

Hilsman stated that in order for intelligence to be "useful and significant" analysis should be frankly and consciously concerned with policy practitioners should have a frame of mind which is instrumental, action-conscious, policy-oriented . The major task is recasting their thought to the context of action adapting their tools to the needs of policy (Marrin, 2016).

Hilsman worked relationships of knowledge and action: examples are the National Security Studies Memorandum (NSSM) in the Nixon and Ford Administrations, and the Presidential Review Memorandum (PRM) in the Carter Administration. Unfortunately, he stated, the PRM/NSSM product line was disbanded in 1980 and appears to have been completely forgotten by both academia and government.

A specific academic discipline was needed. It was in its formative stages for about 20 years from the mid-1980s through to the early 2000s. Through the 2000s the literature has grown in terms of sophistication and abstraction with much additional emphasis on key intelligence concepts and theories. As the field continues to mature improving intelligence studies as an academic discipline will require a return to scholarly fundamentals and best practices in order to create a cumulative, comprehensive, and influential body of disciplinary knowledge for future scholars and practitioners to learn from and contribute to.

Intelligence Studies are the study of the theory and practice of applying information gathered (by both open and clandestine methods) for the purpose of strategic planning, (criminal) investigation, and policy implementation by governments, law enforcement agencies, and business (Moore, 2008)

Scientific Researchers vs Intelligence Analysts: both try to comprehend the world sometimes with strikingly similar way sometimes with very different methods and materials.

Intelligence Analysis, as a political science, examines all of the elements that impact upon the practice of politics, nationally and globally specific sectors of interest are: comparative intelligence, Theory and Applied Intelligence Analysis, Intelligence Policy and Administration, Intelligence and Media, Ethics in Intelligence, Intelligence and the Law, Intelligence and the Executive Branch.

Intelligence education might focus on basic skills, such as: the relationship between Intelligence theory and practice, policy focus, administration and management, strategic planning/futures thinking, risk and vulnerability assessment.

Some factors of influence can be:

- political bureaucracy (i.e. inter-agencies relationships)
- organization theory on: communication processes
- routinized procedures, promotion of specific types of analysis
- psychological factors (cognitive dissonance and other biases)
- historical contingency
- technological change
- demands from politicians and policymakers
- threat perceptions internal vs. external threats
- changes in the international system (i.e., the end of the cold war)

Intelligence Analysis, as a cognitive process basically involves information processing, information evaluation, judgment making. It means the basic skills of: critical thinking, thinking dispositions, epistemological beliefs, conceptual change, information retrieval, reasoning, group behavior, practice based learning, persuasiveness, self-efficacy, rationality, reception theory, dual process mind, thinking styles, competence evaluation.

Intelligence Analysis, as a social science, makes sense to international relations. Warfare and peacekeeping, the resources at stake are essentially social.

Both Social Scientist and Intelligence Analyst create, evaluate and test hypotheses as part of a rigorous, structured approach to analysis. "Intelligence Analysis is rooted in the methodologies and epistemologies of the social science". "Using formal methods had the potential to enable an analytic audit trail" (Marrin, 2011). "The central task of the intelligence officer, historian, and social scientist is to fit facts into meaningful patterns establishing their relevance bearing to the problem at hand" (Knorr, 1964).

As both the study and practice of intelligence analysis incorporates more esplicit references to social science methodology; greater emphasis is being placed on structured analytical techniques as a mechanism for embedding social science methodologies within analytical practices (Marrin, 2011).

Structured analytic techniques provide analysts with simplified frameworks for doing analysis consisting of a checklist derived from best practices in application of the scientific method to social science" (AA.VV., 2011).

But, differently than a Social Sciece, Intelligence analysis, as produced in governments, has an active audience of policy officials looking for help in making decisions, and has access to information that was collected secretly (sometimes illegal if necessary for the purpose). Intelligence analyst is required to be predictive, for crucial needs to act lives in a world of spotty data often looks for particularities, instead of regularities in human behavior (Agrell & Treverton, 2015).

THE INTELLIGENCE CYCLE

The complex phases in which the information security activity is articulated are called "Intelligence Cycle", consisting in 6 steps: planning and direction, collection, processing and analysis, dissemination (Dall'Acqua, 2018). It is a cycle because there is no solution of continuity between the response to needs and the new request for information derive from the previous elaboration.

The phases are as following reported.

Figure 9.

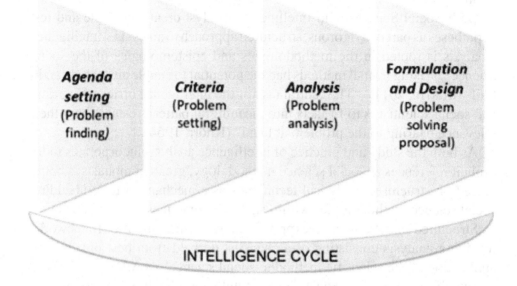

Planning and Direction

Figure 10.

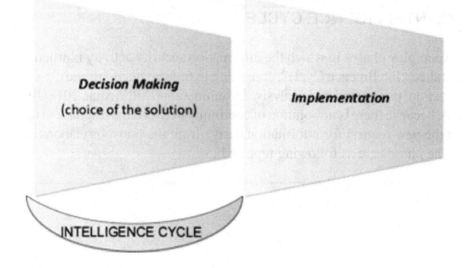

The intelligence cycle is caused by a management decisionthe products of intelligence analysis can assist in developing strategic plans to tactkle current problems and to prepare for anticipating ones. Once the objectives set out, a planning and organizational resourcesoccur. The project planincludesthe agreed objectives, the scope, a timeline, the sequence of activities and a list of the resources.

The strategic areas are set by identifying and ranking in priority levels of the policy areas of service and what information is desired, so set by the heads of the intelligence service and political bodies and, where appropriate, military they serve. The type and content of information that is available and the availability and reliability of sources and channels of communication is studied (AA.VV., 2017b).

The Intelligence contribution to the problem situations is:

- problem (or opportunity) identification (Problem finding)
- problem classification (Problem setting)
- problem decomposition (Problem analysis) and from not-programmed to programmed problems (refined problem analysis)
- problem ownership (accountability)

Collection

Collection management is the process that aligns intelligence needs with information collection and processing capabilities and assets within the various intelligence collection disciplines.

Decision-maker collects information overtly (openly) and covertly (secretly). Reading foreign newspapers and magazine articles, listening to foreign radio, and watching overseas television broadcasts are examples of "overt" (or open) sources for us. Other information sources can be "covert" (or secret). such as information collected with listening devices and hidden cameras. We can even use space-age technology like satellite photography. For instance, some analysts could actually view how many airplanes are present at a foreign military base by looking at a picture taken from a satellite in space.

The collection management process answers the needs of intelligence consumers while making the most economical and effective use of intelligence collection resources. As such, collection management has two distinct functions:

- Collection Resource Management

- Collection Operations Management.

Collection resource management aligns intelligence needs and priorities with available resource management while considering budgetary constraints. On the other hand, collection operations management assigns specific collection tasks to a specific intelligence discipline or a specific system in order to make the most economic and effective use of the collection assets available.

Collection of Raw Information/Data are driven by requirements and priorities. Ability to collect is critical to intelligence quality and, therefore, whether the Intelligence is actionable. The key questions and challenges are:

- who collects information that would become intelligence?
- How is information collected (methodolody)?
- How much information can or should be collected?
- What is the value of the information collected?
- How is information processed?
- What is the role of the analyst in this stage? Is it impartial? Does analysts have an agenda?

Analysis and Processing

The analysis is a central element of the intelligence cycle to provide the users with analysed and assessed information (intelligence knowledge management) to help in decision-making to uncover and define possible threats, risks and challenges (for a decision maker, a company, a State). It is the step by which intelligence is produced from data information. It consists of three steps (Velanquez Hurtado, 2016):

- **recording of information** for comparison with other items by hand. The *integration* of data from different sources is based on a fundamental principle of intelligence: never accept a single information authority. It is getting a synergy where the combination of information from different means of obtaining a whole is most relevant and scope of the information each separately. To describe the work of the departments of analysis. Integration can be a daunting and complex task when data from numerous sources have varied, so it is necessary to provide that much data and documents submitted to the lower levels of protection are spread horizontally among other analysts and departments.

- **assessment of information** in order to determine the value of intelligence; The *evaluation* of the data is to discriminate which contribute to meeting the information requirements formulated in terms of reliability of sources, validity, timeliness, relevance, relevance and usefulness.
- **interpretation of information** concerning other information and intelligence hand in order to reach a conclusion as to its meaning.. The *interpretation* of the data has the dual aim of determining what is accurate and what is relevant to meet the political needs, which are usually alike, explanation and understanding of the phenomenon analyzed as a forecast about its consequences and predictable evolution. The interpretation is the task of experts in the field of analysis (politics, economics, technology, military, and terrorism) possesses both knowledge and sufficient capacity for imagination and creativity to relate data, predicts events, and get into the mind of enemy.

During this phase, there is an open risk of information overload. Policy makers must determine where technology end and human effort begins. The key questions and challenges are:

- Who compiles the raw information/data?
- When is enough?
- Who does the anaysis and what is its value?
- How much are biases a threat?
- What information to share?

The analysis is performed in three phases (Hurtado, 2016):

- The **evaluation** of the data is to discriminate which contribute to meeting the information requirements formulated in terms of reliability of sources, validity, timeliness, relevance, relevance and usefulness.
- The **integration** of data from different sources is based on a fundamental principle of intelligence: never accept a single information authority. It is getting a synergy where the combination of information from different means of obtaining a whole is most relevant and scope of the information each separately. To describe the work of the departments of analysis. Integration can be a daunting and complex task when data from numerous sources have varied, so it is necessary to provide that

Table 2. Intelligence analysis Techniques

Type	Meaning
Strategic analytical techniques	They consist in the analysis of the capabilities of an organization, the aims of the organization itself, the characteristics of the environment in which the organization moves, in order to determine its strategic planning
Competitor analysis techniques	these methodologies concern the value chain in terms of supply and necessity, trying to identify inconsistencies or gaps to be exploited strategically by the organization conducting the analysis
Environmental analysis techniques	*this analysis is carried out observing external elements, considering how these elements can play, an active role in the evolution of a situation, elaborating strategies that can take into account, the presence of external constraints, taking advantage of them*
Evolution analysis techniques	*through these techniques the rules that describe the life of events, products or technologies apply to predict possible scenarios in which context can be highlighted*
Financial analysis techniques	*they concern the financial status of the organizations used to indicate which strategic investments may be, in order to determine the optimal management of funds/actions according to the expected change*

much data and documents submitted to the lower levels of protection are spread horizontally among other analysts and departments.

- The **interpretation** of the data, with the dual aim of determining what is accurate and what is relevant to meet the political needs, which are usually alike, explanation and understanding of the phenomenon analyzed as a forecast about its consequences and predictable evolution. The interpretation is the task of experts in the field of analysis (politics, economics, technology, military, and terrorism) possesses both knowledge and sufficient capacity for imagination and creativity to relate data, predicts events, and get into the mind of enemy.

An example of analytical methods is the National Intelligence Model (NIM) of the United Nations Office on Drugs and Crime (UNODC) which corroborates informed strategic and/or operational decision-making and the development of professional knowledge in effective proactive law enforcement techniques.

Dissemination

The next phase of the intelligence cycle is diffusion or dissemination and use of intelligence, which is the result of all intelligence activities. To be useful,

Figure 11. Types of strategic analysis

DESCRIPTIVE ANALYSIS
(in progress)

EXPLANATORY ANALYSIS
(motivation)

PREDICTIVE ANALYSIS
(development)

it must be reported properly and in time the commander, his older and to those who need state (AA.VV., 2017b).

After reading the final analysis and learning the answer to the original question, the policymaker may come back with more questions. Then the whole process starts over again.

The "CIA Analytic Thinking and Presentation for Intelligence Producers" Guideline AA.VV (2000). draws a detail of the requisites needed to prepare a presentation that correctly summarizes the activity carried out. from the analyst in the previous phases of work. The presentation according to the manual can be enriched by rewarding moments if it becomes an instrument for the analyst to assert his abilities in public.

The fundamental concepts highlighted in the manual are directly linked to the needs of the decision-making level to which the presentation will be exposed. Depending on these needs, the following conditions emerge: to be able to read the presentation in a format already known to avoid distracting attention from the content; having very little time available and inversely proportional to the importance of the content.

Strategic analysis reports, depending on requirements and objectives, are:

- Early warning notifications/intelligence notifications: new or recent changes, trends and developments in the environment, which can be thematic or geographical
- Threat assessments analyse and evaluate the threat of criminal phenomena. They can focus on organized crime groups, specific crime areas or regions

- Risk assessment reports describe the evaluation of potential risks, where the assessment of likelihood, impact and related vulnerabilities is added to the threat assessment
- Situation reports are mainly descriptive. Their objective is to provide a detailed overview of a topic

A key figure within the Intelligence process is that of the analyst, who, especially in the era in which we live, finds himself carrying out an increasingly complex and specialized role. The immense amount of raw data and information with which he finds himself working makes the analyst become the backbone of all modern intelligence. The analyst is the figure that takes care of transforming the raw data, assumed thanks to different information channels, into material suitable for being understood and used by the management level, ie by those figures, so-called decision makers, who, within an organization, they are responsible for defining strategies or making choices. The Intelligence Analyst participates in the policy decision - making cycle at various points: in the obvious phase of analysis and reporting, but also in the data collection phase determining the type of information necessary for that specific problem, and in the planning phase, determining the type of analysis required. According to Malfanti (2014), the analysis methods are "systematic criteria established and defined over time to manage and organize information in order to develop knowledge and make decisions". The analyst's task, therefore, is to organize, verify and make information easily understandable. Technological tools, on the other hand, can be divided into two categories: a) Tools for understanding and processing data: as for example image management software or software for processing and translating texts in rare languages; b) Tools that allow you to highlight relationships within large amounts of data, where otherwise the match would not be possible.

The analyst participates in the intelligence cycle in different phases, starting from the data collection phase, determining the type of information necessary for that particular problem, the analysis and reporting phase. Particularly in the data collection phase, various problems are raised related to the information to be found

THE OSCE MODEL (ILP)

Following, we propose an intepretative framework of analysis. It's a modern and proactive law enforcement model, and a realistic alternative to traditionally reactive forms of policing for OSCE participating States. The Intelligence-led policing model ILP, which has already been adopted in a number of countries in recent years with promising results, combines intelligence gathering, evaluation and analysis with informed decision-making procedures and mechanisms, thus providing more efficient and effective management of national law enforcement (see Figure 12).

Tasking based on policy, strategic and operational plans, emerging threats or identified needs the national, regional or local law enforcement management tasks and provides directions to the analysis management distributes tasks to individual analysis departments, units or individual analysts. The tasking phase requires close co-operation between the analysts and political decision-makers. They need to agree on:the subject of inquiry, objectives, aim, scope, timeline and form of reporting, including the dissemination and recipient of the intelligence product The analyst needs to be clear on the expectations and the intent of the (political) decision-makers.

Analysis: Following directions and tasking from management or requests from investigators analysts develop intelligence in line with a defined intelligence process. The analysis process generates strategic and operational **(criminal) intelligence products.** The products are used as a basis for developing strategic and operational plans for supporting investigations and other law enforcement operations for prioritizing and allocating human/technical resources

Decision-making: Each country maintains a decision-making structure at the national, regional and local levels where analysis reports/intelligence products are used as a basis for decisions

The **operational policing areas** generate data, information and intelligence that are forwarded through clearly defined communication channels and stored in databases that allow for further analysis

DECISION-MAKING PROCESS WITHIN THE FOREIGN AND SECURITY POLICY: HISTORICAL CASES

Decision-making in foreign policy refers to the choices that individuals, groups and coalitions make that influence the actions of a nation on the international stage. Since the international arena is characterized by strong uncertainty, also linked to anarchy, the understanding of how choices are made allows us to understand and predict the results emerging in the scenario itself.

Figure 12. The OSCE intelligence-led policing model (AA.VV., 2017b)

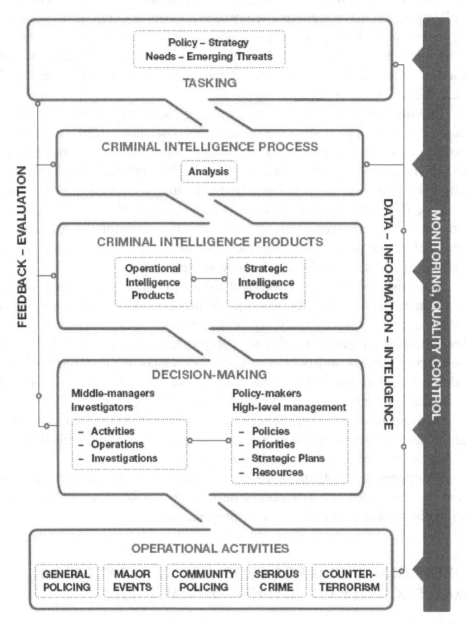

The process of analysis is the essence of many foreign policy decisions. It consists in an interactive setting and consisting of a sequence of decisions. It has enriched understanding of the diversionary use of force in international bargaining and negotiation, coalition formation, terrorists' decisions.

In the early 1990s Alex Mintz and colleagues developed a so called **"Poliheuristic theory"**.

Poliheuristic theory is uniquely positioned to contribute to progress in the study of world politics, and is related to the Applied Decision Analysis (ADA), an analytic procedure which can be applied to all levels of analysis in foreign policy decision-making:

- the leader (i.e. the president)
- the group (i.e. the Congress)
- the coalition (i.e.parliamentary democracy)

The theory is based on five main processing characteristics of decision-making. It examines the determinants of foreign policy decisions, such as the decision environment (time constraints, ambiguity - uncertainty, stress / risk), psychological factors that shape decisions (belief systems, emotions, the personality of the leader, leadership style, miscalculations and misperceptions), the effect of international-domestic factors (deterrence to act, the arms race, the regime type of the adversary, strategic surprise, economic conditions, public opinion, electoral cycles on foreign policy decisions making), and environmental factors. Foreign policy, like domestic policy, is formulated within the state unlike domestic policy. it is directed and must be implemented in the environment external to that state.

In the case of the USA, ideologies, beliefs and inclinations of the last three presidents have been totally different, both in domestic and foreign politics. For example, the approach that Bush had towards the Muslim world, influenced by the events of September 11, was one of distrust and prevention with those who could have relations with Al Qaeda. It was an obvious aggressive foreign policy, legitimized as defensive. Instead, Obama has activated a more pacifist policy, aimed at promoting good relations with the Muslim world, also taking into account the presence of a heterogeneous electorate in the USA, mostly Muslim. As for Trump, his foreign policy appears, in some respects, unpredictable, without compromise. Even his strong, direct and little diplomatic language proves it, and at times many media have called him provocative at the international level.

Table 3. Determinants of foreign policy

Levels	Types
Individual level	• Leadership style • Ideologically-driven (i.e. beliefs, attitudes, motives • and passions) • Pragmatic (i.e. flexible and openminded) • Personality (i.e Emotional vs Rational) • Foreign policy can be different under different leaders. For example: Leaders may perceive the Muslim world differently
Domestic level	• Effects of domestic dynamics on foreign policy • National and Societal Characteristics size, wealth, economic system, political accountability, democratic culture • Role of bureaucracy, public opinion, media
Interstate level	• Historical rivalry or friendship between states • Changing nature of relations in bilateral relations
Regional level	• Effects of changing regional dynamics on foreign policy
Global level	• Effects of global events and transformations on foreign policy • Global communication networks and technology • Global terror

A Case of Effects of Domestic Dynamics on Foreign Policy: Turkish-Greek Relations After the 1999 Earthquake

Although Greece and Turkey are both members of NATO, there are perhaps no two allied neighboring nations whose dealings have been marked with so much conflict and mistrust. Greece was under Turkish rule for centuries and fought a bitter conflict for independence against Ottoman rule in the 1820's. A century later, the republic of Turkey was formed after Turkish forces drove Greeks from Anatolia, and relations since then have been plagued by conflict.

Greek-Turkish relations had been improving slowly for several months, but it took earthquakes in both countries to push them toward a more heart-felt friendship. Each sent rescue teams to help the other, and their gestures were greeted by waves of ecstatic publicity and popular emotion. ''I think we're in the middle of a new phenomenon that you could call seismic diplomacy or earthquake diplomacy,'' said Nicholas Burns, the United States Ambassador to Greece. Images that people saw on TV had tremendous political symbolism, and there's an opportunity for both sides to build on that.

Greek and Turkish diplomats met in Athens to plan cultural exchanges and discuss cooperation in tourism, the environment, trade and other areas. While they were meeting, Turks observed the anniversary of their 1922 military triumph over Greece with a restraint they had never shown before.

In the wake of the Turkish and Greek earthquakes, what some reporters described as the 'earthquake' or 'seismic' diplomacy between the two neighbours raised expectations that Greek-Turkish relations may enter a new era of cooperation. A series of bilateral meetings, scheduled before the earthquakes, registered considerable progress on such topics as cultural ties, border security, as well as fighting terrorism and organized crime. At the same time, however, as some commentators and officials in both countries have observed, there exists a wide divergence of interests between the two neighbours (Stephen Kinzer, 1999)

A Case of a Role of Bureaucracy: The 1st March 2003 Motion in the Turkish Parliament Preventing US Troops from Entering Iraq Through Turkish Soil

On March 2, 2003, the Turkish Parliament rejected a measure that would have allowed thousands of American combat troops to use the country as a base for an attack. The vote also quashed the possibility that Turkish troops would enter northern Iraq, a prospect that many there, especially the country's Kurds, regarded with dread.

Turkey, one of the America's closest allies and a member of NATO, is a secular Muslim democracy whose support in the region the Bush administration has craved. Indeed, American officials have called Turkey a model for the type of system they are hoping an invasion of Iraq would help bring elsewhere in the Middle East.

The defeat seemed to surprise Turkey's leaders, who only hours earlier had predicted that Parliament would approve the measure. Prime Minister Abdullah Gul, and the chief of the governing Justice and Development Party, Recep Tayyip Erdogan, had endorsed the resolution, and both men had urged their party, which controls a large majority of the Parliament, to support it.

As well as the defeat stunned American officials, who had been confident that Turkey's leaders would be able to persuade the members of their party to support the measure. American ships had already begun unloading heavy equipment at Turkish ports in anticipation of a victory, and two dozen vessels were idling off the coast.

This situation posed immediate military problems for American officials, who had been counting on Turkey's support to bring as many as 62,000 American troops into the country to build a northern front. A senior Pentagon official publically said at once that the American military would be able to stage the operation without Turkey's help, but most military analysts agreed that it would be extremely difficult without a northern base.

The American request had placed Turkey's lawmakers in a difficult position; polls here indicate that as many as 9 of 10 Turks oppose involvement in a war against Iraq. In the end, the resolution failed because nearly 100 members of the governing party appeared to have voted against the measure or to have abstained.

The Turkish vote threw into question for a while the military strategy that devised to overwhelm the forces of President Saddam Hussein. American military commanders wanted to begin an attack from Turkey that would pin down Iraqi forces in the north and keep them away from the main American force driving from the south (Filkins, 2003).

A Case of Effects of Changing Regional Dynamics on Foreign Policy: Effects of the Syrian Refugee Crisis on Turkish Foreign Policy

The Syrian refugee situation in Turkey has become an integration and security issue with social, economic and political dimensions. As a result, it has been generally accepted that a policy based only on providing the basic needs of the refugees is unsustainable. Upon realization of this, the institutions tasked with administering the issue have been working on this dimension.

Turkey began to reform and regulate laws in accordance with the European Union laws as a process of alignment and harmonization. Under the National Action Plan for Adoption of Acquis on Asylum and Migration, the required steps were taken, and a timetable was introduced in line with the EU laws and regulations with regards to the migration and asylum policies. Readmission Agreement (2013), Joint Action Plan (2015) and the EU-Turkey Deal Statement (2016) came into force with the contributions and efforts of Turkey and the EU.

As a result of this joint action, Turkey-EU relations were renewed in a more cooperative approach fulfilling partnership and cooperation objectives, after a period of ups and downs within the long history of Turkey's accession process.

From the Turkish perspective, the increasing instability in the region and Turkey's isolation from the EU have made the Turkish public think pessimistically about the relations with the EU (Çetin et. al., 2017).

A Case of Global Terror: The US Foreign Policy Changed Drastically After 9/11 Global Economic Crisis

In the history of humankind, there has been no other single terrorist act like the 9/11 attacks which have had such a negative impact on the economy of countries worldwide and at the same time on the emotional condition of billions of people around the world. Paradoxically, international tourism and international terrorism have some issues in common. Both have global implications - involving people from different countries and use travel and communications facilities (Soenmez, 1998).

The negative economic consequences of the US tourism industry caused by the crisis have had an immediate affect on global tourism economies due to the tight interrelation of international tourism industries. The first shock following the attacks has resulted in a deep market recession. Besides that, governments, international organizations and tourism and travel companies were forced to work on emergency crisis management plans in order to find adequate solutions for the industry's recovery, as well as to prevent similar attacks in the future. Due to the geographical location of the United States air transportation was one of the few vital "bridges" with the rest of the world. The impact of the terrorist attacks on the travel industry was so enormous that without federal support it would not have been able to survive. Economic, security and legislation measures were undertaken by the United States government and other official authorities and tourism institutions to combat the consequences of the crisis and help the domestic tourism economy to recover from the crisis (Bysyuk, 2010)

LABORATORY FOR PRACTITIONERS

This section is dedicated to a series of exercises, useful to train Intelligence practitioners. More the cultural path of the practioner is advanced, more success of the application is granted.

Exercise 1: Policy Cycle Steps Awareness

The purpose of this exercise is to understand what Policy cycle means, and to let practitioners be aware of every single management path. The grid to fill is related to a part of the Policy Cycle steps.

The practitioners start with a field of analysis application better close to the daily life, such as the investigative process of a doctor with the patient, to extend the analysis to the educational system, anyway indirectly near to a personal experience, such as the management path of a decision by a Minister of the Education. Furthermore, the same exercise is applied into a crucial political sector, such as a Defence Minister Finally the practioner should compare his/her answers.

Assignment: *First part: you are a Doctor and you have in front of you a Patient (think to a specific case). Fill the steps according to possible actions. Take into account the variables: ANAMNESIS, DIAGNOSIS, PROGNOSIS, FINAL CHECK. Second part: you are the Minister of the Education. Repeat the same exercise. Third part: you are the Defense Minister. Repeat the same exercise. Fourth part: compare your answers. What's similar? What's different? What lacks?*

Ex Ante Evaluation (In Synthesis)

- **Agenda setting** (Problem finding): acknowledgment of the problem
- **Criteria** (Problem setting): the methodology to define the problem. **COMMENT: attention: talking about methodological criteria**
- **Analysis** (Problem analysis): break down the main problem into secondary problems
- **Formulation and Design** (Problem solving proposal)

In Itinere Evaluation (In Synthesis)

- **Decision Making:** choice of the solution. It induces the decision maker to assume specific behaviors and actions
- **Implementation**

Final Questions 1

- what's the main problem in your opinion (your first account)?
- what's the human factor?
- what's the technical factor?
- what's the rules factor?
- what's the fact without a judgment?
- who can have a possible emotional involvement and what can the possible consequence be?

- who can have possible bias and what can the possible consequence be?
- what can the negative aspects be, the reasons why it cannot work?
- what can positive aspects, benefits and opportunities be?
- thcrc arc possible creative ideas, innovations?
- what are possible rules/organizations of proposed actions?

Final Questions 2 (A Comparison Between Different Study Cases)

- what's similar?
- what's different?
- what lacks?

As an example, below we report some of the main answers of groups of two/ three-person teams. It's useful to understand the real difficulty of analysis for someone, even if the practitioners understood the theory.

At the end of the exercises, the practitioners have shared their answers each other, and optimized every own point of view and interpretation.

Ex Ante Evaluation

1) **Agenda setting** (Problem finding): acknowledgment of the problem

2) **Criteria** (Problem setting): the methodology to define the problem. **COMMENT: attention: talking about methodological criteria**

3) **Analysis** (Problem analysis): break down the main problem into secondary problems

4) **Formulation and Design** (Problem solving proposal)

In Itinere Evaluation

5) **Decision Making:** choice of the solution. It induces the decision maker to assume specific behaviors and actions

GROUP 1: Patient feels ill. Patient booked an appointment. Patient has stomachaches.
GROUP 2: The patient shows multiple red blisters on his skin. Moreover, the patient is affected by a deep pricking, abdominal pain and high temperature. According to these symproms. We assume this is varicella
GROUP 3: The patient affirms to be in a feverish state, accompanied by a general feeling of tiredness and grave itching caused by numerous rashes on the entire body
GROUP 4: the patient suffers of headaches and has difficulty in concentrating
GROUP 5: questions: what's your problem? Where does it hurt? How long do you feel pain?
GROUP 6: call to the operations center by a witness who saw a machine collide against the wall
GROUP 7: the patient has a lack of pronunciation
GROUP 8: ask: what is the problem, when it happened, in which part of the body manifests itself and what symptoms are present
GROUP 9: baby with fever for a couple of days with a wet nose and dry cough. Skin rash
GROUP10: the patient shows up in the clinic claiming to have various illnesses: headaches, difficulty breathing, swollen lymph nodes, dry cough, and balance problem. His medical record reports chronic heart disease

6)   Implementation

GROUP 3: How long the patient has had a stomach (.....ache?). Look at the patient medical history. Ask for any other symptoms. Take patient temperature. Enquire about patient diet.
GROUP 1: How first decision was to proceed with a blood test. In fact, our first purpose was either to find traces of some virus or, in alternative, some proof to exclude another pathology.
GROUP 2: to verify if the fever is high and persists for more than 3 days and if rashes continue to spread on the body. Depending on the patient's response, we can identify these symptoms as an infections decease or as flu combined with another factor that caused the rashes
GROUP 4: direct communication of the situation by the patient, medical exams (official documents), observation of the patient
GROUP 5: analysis of symptoms. Some questions to deepen his living style
GROUP 6: the nurse asks the witness to describe the scene and what he sees on the spot. The witness states that the patient is unconscious.
GROUP 7: the direct conversation with the patient (as the child speaks). Interview with the patient's parents
GROUP 8: clinical history of the patient. List of possible causes of the problem (diseases). The patient visit to focus on the cause of the illness (streamline the list). Determine the most probable causes and choose the exams accordingly
GROUP 9: possible questions: how many days do you have symptoms? Does the fever continue to increase? Does conjunctivitis have white dots in the mouth? etc
GROUP 10: based on my previous experience, on my studies and on the patient's words, I try to outline a diagnostic profile. To ascertain the veracity and intensity of what the patient complains, I prescribe specific tests

GROUP 1: he only has stomach pains after meals. Patient had started taking the contraceptive pill 3 weeks ago.
GROUP 2: A patient affected by varicella shows a huge variety of of symptoms. The main features of this pathology are, of course, blisters and deep pricking. Beyond, these ones, we have noticed that the patient suffers great headache, difficulty in breathing and insomnia.
GROUP 3: the patient has shown a high fever for a few days, accompanied by continuous itching and general tiredness. To resolve the patient's problem, first we need to alleviate the fever and then we can see how the patient responds to specific treatments for the skin rashes
GROUP 4: lack of good sleep, stress, possible sight problems, overworking, possible wrong medications, wrong dosages
GROUP 5: the doctor focused on single symptoms to his analysis and to exclude some problems
GROUP 6: which type of ambulance and team are available and more suitable. Furthermore, if there is a need to call additional assistance.
GROUP 7: possible neurological/physical problems (malformations, etc.). Psychological causes (possible trauma). Educational causes. Possible difficulties in bilingualism
GROUP 8: break down disease based on the symptoms present. Contain the problem with actions aimed at reducing secondary or more urgent symptoms
GROUP 9: possible exclusions of diseases based on some observations.
GROUP10: from the executed exams I find out what the pathology the patient suffers from, and I understand that only a part of the symptoms he is diagnosed are directly related to the main pathology. The others can be labeled as mild

Exercise 2: Policy Cycle Steps Awareness

This exercise is an extension of the previous one. It includes a SWOT analysis for each question, liniting the analysis only to the Ex Ante evaluation.

GROUP 1: Make a food diary to track foods - stomach pains. Refer to a nutritionist. Stomach pain medication.
GROUP 2: In dealing with varicella, we had to consider an antiviral medicine as much as immuno-globulins or aspirin. Another possible proposal to solve the problem would be an increasing personal hygienic care.
GROUP 3: Recommend the use of Tylenol for the feverish state and tiredness, accompanied by a lotion to reduce the itchiness, as the symptoms seems to correspond to chicken pox virus
GROUP 4: temporary solution (in terms of medications) and deeep investigation of the possible causes
GROUP 5: on the basis of data collected before, the doctor formulates a first proposal to face the problem (diagnosis)
GROUP 6: send the appropriate team with a doctor on board the ambulance
GROUP 7: subjecting the child to linguistic, psychological, cognitive and medical tests to identify the origin of the problem. Interview with parents: know the linguistic environment in which the child is inserted. Diagnosis: the child has difficulty in pronunciation related to bilingualism and poor exposure to the second language
GROUP 8: formulate a clearer picture of the patient by reducing the options, assuming the consequences of the possible intake of specific drugs and, if necessary, admitting the patient and/or providing for surgery and/or psychological assistance
GROUP 9: drugs to treat symptoms, isolation due to a danger of infection
GROUP10: the diagnosis is bronchial pneumonia of medium intensity,

GROUP 1: Persuade patient about health benefits of medication and dieting
GROUP 2: Considering that we are in front of a baby, our final decision is to prescribe him a complete cycle of acyclovir. In fact, aspirin would be the wrong choice because the patient is pretty young and this decision could imply contra-indications
GROUP 3: Assume Tylenol for 1/2 times a day to reduce fever, and general tiredness, lotion for rashes
GROUP 4: prescribing medical checks (exams), advising the patient about a healthier routine, checking the new medications effects, if necessary, changing the medication, on the basis of the medical exams' results, change the procedure or renew it
GROUP 5: the doctor advises the patient to take specific drugs, take cure of himself, not to smoke, have some rest
GROUP 6: send the appropriate team with a doctor on board the ambulance
GROUP 6: we reach the site of the accident and notice that the patient is still unconscious. We observe that the lower limbs are embedded, the reason why the team decides to call the fire brigades
GROUP 7: therapeutic path with the specialist
GROUP 8: the example of cerebral hemorrhage: an immediate admission is decided
GROUP 9: the child aged less than 3 years and has a two-day fever, with symptoms typical of colds and white spots in the mouth. This leads to thinking about the beginning of measles

The practitioners have to design a final flowchart of actions.

Assignment: *With your team, prepare a flowchart that shows your actual supply process, and then indicate where the problems are and what actions might be taken to ensure that the appropriate <u>prevention of a crime</u> is made available to a political decision-maker to propose a new defence law. Before preapring the flowchart, fill these issues.*

GROUP 1: Describe medication.
GROUP 2: An acyclovir has been administrated as soon as the patient has arrived to the hospital. Moreover, the kid has to avoid school for one week.
GROUP 3: The patient has taken Tylenol for 5 days and is continuing to use the lotion
GROUP 4: giving the patient the necessary prescription/documents, practical hints/advises for a healthier life, calling the patient in for a new visit, comparing the medication effects to those of patients with similar conditions, reading the exams results ad confirm or change the procedure
GROUP 5: the doctor requires weekly checks to control if the patient follos his adises and to monito if the cure is working
GROUP 6: after the intervention of the firefighters the patient is free. We stabilize it and transport it to the nearest trauma-center
GROUP 7: propose to parents to expose the child more to the second language. Ask for teacher collaboration. Diction exercises
GROUP 8: during the admission, the patient is constantly monitored to verify the persistence or not of the symptoms. Prescribed absolute physical and cognitive rest and physiotherapy to solve balance problems due to symptoms
GROUP 9: medicines to lower fever and syrup to relieve cough
GROUP 10: the patient is hospitalized and discharged after 7 days and the administration of a course of antibiotics

1) **Problem finding:** acknowledgment of the problem.
   a. Describe the Strenght points in the action to find it
   b. Describe the Weakness points in the action to find it
   c. Describe the Opportunities in the action to find it
   d. Describe the Threats in the action to find it
   e. Synthetize your meta-analysis
2) **Problem setting**: the methodology to define the problem
   a. Describe the Strenght points in the action to define it
   b. Describe the Weakness points in the action to define it
   c. Describe the Opportunities in the action to define it
   d. Describe the Threats in the action to define it
   e. Synthetize your meta-analysis
3) **Problem analysis:** break down the main problem into secondary problems
   a. Describe the Strenght points in the action to decompose it
   b. Describe the Weakness points in the action to decompose it
   c. Describe the Opportunities in the action to decompose it
   d. Describe the Threats in the action to decompose it
   e. Synthetize your meta-analysis
4) **Formulation and Design**
   a. Describe the Strenght points in the action to design it
   b. Describe the Weakness points in the action to design it
   c. Describe the Opportunities in the action to design it
   d. Describe the Threats in the action to design it
   e. Synthetize your meta-analysis
      Final action 1: Identify the human factors in the study case
      Final action 2: Identify the tehnical factors in the study case

REFERENCES

AA.VV. (2011). *Committee on Behavioral and Social Science Research to Improve Intelligence Analysis for National Security. National Research Concil, Intelligence Analysis for Tomorrow: Advances from the Behavioral and Social Science*. National Academies Press.

AA.VV. (2012). *Glossario Intelligence: il linguaggio degli organismi informativi.* Presidenza del consiglio dei ministri Rivista italiana di Intelligence.

Agrell & Treverton. (2015). *National Intelligence and Science*. Oxford University Press.

AA.VV. (2000). *The CIA Analytic Thinking and Presentation for Intelligence Producers Guideline*. Retrieved from: https://cryptome.org/cia-ath-pt1.htm

AA.VV. (2017a). *Guidebook, Intelligence-Led Policing* (Vol. 13). Organization for Security and Co-operation in Europe.

AA.VV. (2017b). *Scuola di formazione per i politici del futuro*. Retrieved from: http://www.pollinotour.com/2017/05/03/scuola-di-formazione-per-i-politici-del-futuro/

Arcuri, C. (1990). La trasparenza invisibile. Nuovi diritti di liberta': L'accesso dei cittadini all'informazione. In *Science politiche*. Marietti.

Buse, K., & Young, J. (2006). *Tools to understand the political and policy context & engage with policy makers. Research and Policy in Development*. Overseas Development Institute.

Bysyuk, V. (2010). *Impact of 9/11 Terrorist Attacks on US and International Tourism Development*. Retrieved from website https://www.modul.ac.at/uploads/files/Theses/Bachelor/BYSYUK_Impact_of_9_11_on_US_and_International_Tourism_Development.pdf

Çetin, R. A., Çetin, S., Turan, E., & Hamsioglu, O. (2017). The Impact of the Syrian Refugee Crisis on Turkey-EU Relations. International Journal of Political Studies.

Colebatch, H. K. (2006). What work makes Policy? Policy Sciences, 39(4), 309-321.

Dall'acqua, L. (2019). *Forecasting and managing risk in the health and safety sectors*. Hershey, PA: IGI Global. doi:10.4018/978-1-5225-7903-8

Dall'acqua, L., & Lukos, E. D. (2018). *Improving Business Performance Through Effective Managerial Training Initiatives*. Hershey, PA: IGI Global. doi:10.4018/978-1-5225-3906-3

Dente, B. (2014). *Understanding Policy Decisions*. Springer. doi:10.1007/978-3-319-02520-9

Dunn, W. N. (1994). *Public Policy Analysis: An Introduction*. Prentice Hall.

Filkins, D. (2003*). Threats and resposnes: Ankara; Turkish deputies refuse to accept American troops.* Retrieved from website https://www.nytimes.com/2003/03/02/world/threats-and-responses-ankara-turkish-deputies-refuse-to-accept-american-troops.html

Fleisher, C. S., & Bensoussan, B. E. (2003). *Strategic and Competitive Analysis: Methods And Techniques for Analyzing Business Competition.* Prentice Hall.

Goldman, J. (2011). *Words of Intelligence: An Intelligence Professional's Lexicon for Domestic and Foreign Threats, Security and Professional Intelligence Education Series.* Scarecrow Press.

Kinzer, S. (1999). *Earthquakes Help Warm Greek-Turkish Relations.* Retrieved from website https://www.nytimes.com/1999/09/13/world/earthquakes-help-warm-greek-turkish-relations.html

Knoepfel. (2007). *Public Policy Analysis.* Policy Press, University of Bristol. doi:10.2307/j.ctt9qgz7q

Knorr, E. (1964). *Intelligence and social science.* Princeton: Center of International Studiews, Woodrow Wilson School of Public and International Affairs.

Malfanti, F. (2005). *Il ruolo dell'analista di Intelligence.* Intelligrate – Competitive Intelligence and Data Integration.

Marrin, S. (2016). Improving Intelligence Studies as an Academic Discipline. *Intelligence and National Security, 31*(2), 266–279. doi:10.1080/02684527.2014.952932

Mayer, E., Lee, H., & Peebles, A. (2014, September/October). Multimedia Learning in a Second Language: A Cognitive Load Perspective. *Applied Cognitive Psychology, 28*(5), 653–660. doi:10.1002/acp.3050

Mintz, A., & DeRouen, K. (2010). *Understanding Foreign Policy Decision Making.* Cambridge University Press. doi:10.1017/CBO9780511757761

Monten, J., & Bennett, A. (2010). Models of Crisis Decision Making and the 1990-91 Gulf War. *Security Studies, 19*(3), 486–520. doi:10.1080/09636412.2010.505129

Moore, G. (2008). The View From the Tower: Thoughts on the Emergence of an Academic Discipline and Educational Process for the 21st Century. *10th Annual colloquium on intelligence.*

Ratcliffe, J. H. (2016). *Intelligence-Led policing*. Routledge.

Reverton, G. F. (2006). *Toward a Theory of Intelligence Workshop Report*. National Security Research Division, U.S. Department of Defense.

Soenmez, S.F. (1998). Tourism, terrorism, and political instability. Annals of Tourism Research, 25(2), 416–456.

Steele, R. D. (2000). On Intelligence: Spies and Secrecy in an Open World. *Proceedings of AFCEA 2000.*

Velásquez Hurtado, L. A. (2016). *Colombia and the intelligence cycle in the 21st century, the digital age* (Master's Thesis). Institute of Computer Science, University of Tartu. Available in: https://comserv.cs.ut.ee/home/files/Velasq uez+Hurtado+CyberSecurity+2016.pdf?study=ATILoputoo&reference=0 F5176FB1F90355934306790E8C049BBCD9E422E

Walt, & Gilson. (1994). *Framework for health policy anaylsis*. Retrieved from https://www.researchgate.net/figure/Framework-for-health-policy-analysis-Source-Walt-Gilson-1994-7_fig1_51469060

Waltz, E. (2003). *Knowledge Management in the Intelligence Enterprise*. Artech House Publishers.

ADDITIONAL READING

Kerbel, J., & Olcott, A. (2010). The Intelligence-Policy Nexus: Synthesizing with Clients, Not Analyzing for Customers. *Studies in Intelligence*, *54*(4), 1–13.

Marrin, S., & Davies, P. H. J. (2009). National Assessment by the National Security Council Staff 1968–80: American Experiment in a British Style of Analysis. *Intelligence and National Security*, *24*(5), 644–673. doi:10.1080/02684520903209407

Ratcliffe, J. (2016). *Intelligence-Led policing*. Routledge. doi:10.4324/9781315717579

KEY TERMS AND DEFINITIONS

Decision-Making: Consists of evaluating and selecting one feasible solution from among a set of alternatives. Decision-making process includes recognizing and defining the nature of a decision situation, identifying alternatives, choosing the 'best' [most effective] alternative, putting it into practice.

Foreign Policy: The sum of a state's all (economic, political, cultural) activities outside its borders to promote the domestic values and interests.

Intelligence: The analytical process for specific needs of anticipated knowledge, to allow decision makers to choose and adopt the strategy to be pursued and, consequently, to decide in a timely, convenient, and effective manner; the competitive intelligence regarding the business intelligence, or investigative intelligence applied to the fight against crime.

Intelligence Analyst: Who takes care of transforming raw data, collected through the various information channels, into material suitable for being understood and used by the management level.

Problem Solving: The process of identifying alternative possible courses of action representing solutions.

Chapter 2
Policy–Decision Environment and Cognitive Biases:
Cases Study

ABSTRACT

Cognitive biases are a mistake in reasoning, evaluating, remembering, or other cognitive processes. They are mental errors caused by our simplified information processing strategies, and can be cultural, emotional, or intellectual predispositions toward a certain judgment, organizational bias, and bias that results from one's self-interest. The chapter explores some case studies in the foreign policy decision-making, distinguished in groupthink and polythink types, such as Pearl Harbor, Cuba Missile Crisis, Iraq Invasion of 2003, and post-9/11 environment.

INTRODUCTION

Humans tend to think in certain ways that can lead to systematic deviations from making rational judgments. When evidence is lacking or ambiguousanalysts evaluate hypotheses by applying their general ackground knowledgeconcerning the nature of systems and behavior

In the first instance, we need to know that there are two general modes of thinking, intuitive and reflective. The study about the differences in the two forms of thought has been expanded in recent years (Chaiken and Trope, 1999; Myers, 2002). In 2002, Kahneman & Frederick made the Prospect

DOI: 10.4018/978-1-7998-1562-4.ch002

Theory, which postulates that there are two systems called 1 and 2 that guide decision making process. At present, there is considerable consensus on the features that distinguish these two types of cognitive processes (Stanovich and West, 2000).

On the one hand, the system 1 allows the formulation of intuitive judgments, thinking, associations and feeling. The operations of system 1 are fast, automatic, effortless performed from associations, and are difficult to control or modify. This system is used when we drive a car, play football or have a bath that is in daily routines where we are not consciously focusing but simply we do them. On the other hand, the system 2 includes consciously controlled judgments, deliberate and sequential reasoning. The operations of system 2 are slower, serial, are made with effort, and are deliberately controlled. They are also relatively flexible and can be checked by potential rules. This system is at work when we need to pay attention to learn new activity such as dancing salsa.

Following this line, Kahneman (2002) showed that people also use emotional heuristic to take risks or make conservative choices. Affective reactions would allow heuristics be more accessible, generating impressions that would condition the system 2 when is taking judgments or decisions.

How is the work of neuroscientists, cognitive scientists and psychologists useful to understand foreign policy decision-making?

Table 1. Reasoning

How we ought to reason	How we actually reason
Deductive logic Probability, Statistics Decision theory Game theory	The mind processes information in ways that mimic these formal models of reasoning and decision making

Cognitive biases are a mistake in reasoning, evaluating, remembering, or other cognitive processes. They are mental errors caused by our simplified information processing strategies, and can be cultural, emotional or intellectual predisposition toward a certain judgment, organizational bias, and bias that results from one's own self-interest.

Cognitive biases are similar to optical illusions in that the error remains compelling even when one is fully aware of its nature. But awareness of the bias, by itself does not produce a more accurate perception.

These tendencies usually arise from:

- Information processing shortcuts
- The limited processing ability of the brain
- Emotional and moral motivations
- Distortions in storing and retrieving memories
- Social influence
- Preferences and beliefs regardless of contrary information

Figure 1. Academic fields to study cognitive biases

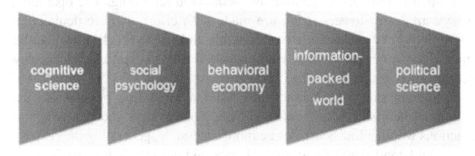

Cognitive biases can cause us big problems along our life. Bias can help us to take a right or effective and quick decision, but many times they produce that we take wrong, illogical or unfounded decision or judgments. Some decisions are made after careful calculation whereas others are more intuitive. Cognitive limitations can often distort information processing

Specifically, the confirmation bias, a type of Pattern- Recognition Biases, is the tendency to selectively search for or interpret information in a way that confirms one´s preconceptions or hypothesis (Jonas et al, 2001). This bias is very common in legal field. For example, a jury has to analysis the different hypothesis and chooses the most likely. However, people sometimes focus only their attention in evidence that confirming their hypothesis and giving more weight to this evidence, and moreover, disconforming evidence is rejected by them. This result in the sentence can be wrong because it is biased. .

Table 2. Most relevant biases groups

Type	Meaning	Examples
PATTERN-RECOGNITION BIASES	Lead us to recognize patterns even where there are none	Once we have formulated a theory, we pay more attention to items that support it, and ignore evidence that disproves it. We pay more attention to highly memorable events. We give more weight to recent events.
STABILITY BIASES	Create a tendency towards inertia in the presence of uncertainty	We take comfort in doing things the same way again and again. We do things a certain way, because that's the way they've always been done. We avoid risks, and punish each other for taking chances that might end in failure.
ACTION-ORIENTED BIASES	Drive us to take less thoughtfully than we should	We feel pressure to take action. We are (sometimes overly) optimistic about results. We dismiss the possibility of negative outcomes. We are overconfident in our ability to influence events. We disregard the impact of chance occurrences.
INTEREST BIASES	Arise in the presence of conflicting incentives, including non-monetary and even purely emotional ones	We create incentives that reward the wrong behavior, or we create conflicting incentives. We have silo thinking. We don't consider the big picture or other people's perspectives. We're motivated to obtain a favorable outcome for ourselves or our unit at the expense of others.
SOCIAL BIASES	Arise from the preference for harmony over conflict	We are deeply influenced by office politics. We support our own groups, our own leaders. We strive to keep people happy instead of challenging them. We expect people to conform to the accepted way of thinking

COGNITIVE BIASES IN NATIONAL AND FOREIGN POLICY DECISION-MAKING

Groupthink

Groupthink, or group thought is the word used in the scientific literature to indicate a pathology of the system of thought exhibited by members of a social group: Individual creativity, originality, autonomy of thought, are all sacrificed in exchange for the pursuit of the values of group cohesion. likewise, those advantages deriving from a reasonable balancing of different or opposing choices and opinions are lost

"Members of a small cohesive group tend to maintain the spirit of the body by unconsciously developing a series of shared illusions and relative norms that interfere with critical thinking and verification of reality" (Janis, 1982, p.35).

Janis also argued that this tendency does not appear to be an isolated phenomenon to a decision-making group at a particular time and within a specific culture, but characterizes each type of group and shows very specific

Table 3. Some simple types of misperception and bias (Source: Krizan, 1999)

TYPE	MEANING
Best-Case Analysis	Optimistic assessment based on cognitive predisposition and general beliefs of how others are likely to behave, or in support of personal or organizational interests or policy preferences.
Conservatism in Probability Estimation	In a desire to avoid risk, tendency to avoid estimating extremely high or extremely low probabilities. Routine thinking. Inclination to judge new phenomena in light of past experience, to miss essentially novel situational elements, or failure to reexamine established tenets. Tendency to seek confirmation of prior held beliefs.
Defensive Avoidance	Refusal to perceive and understand extremely threatening stimuli. Need to avoid painful choices. Leads to wishful thinking.
Denial of Rationality	Attribution of irrationality to others who are perceived to act outside the bounds of one's own standards of behavior or decision making. Opposite of rational-actor hypothesis. Can result from ignorance, mirror imaging, parochialism, or ethnocentrism.
Evoked-Set Reasoning	That information and concern, which dominates one's thinking based on prior experience. One tends to uncritically relate new information to past or current dominant concerns
Excessive Secrecy (Compartmentation)	Over-narrow reliance on selected evidence. Based on concern for operational security. Narrows consideration of alternative views. Can result from or caused organizational parochialism.
Inappropriate Analogies	Perception that an event is analogous to past events based on inadequate consideration of concepts or facts or irrelevant criteria. Bias of "Representativeness".
Ignorance	Lack of knowledge. Can result from prior-limited priorities or lack of curiosity, perhaps based on ethnocentrism, parochialism, and denial of reality, rational-actor hypothesis (see next entry).
Overconfidence in Subjective Estimates	Optimistic bias in assessment. Can result from premature or rapid closure of consideration, or ignorance.
Prematurely Formed Views	These spring from a desire for simplicity and stability, and lead to premature closure in the consideration of a problem.
Presumption of Unitary Action by Organizations	Perception that behavior of others is more planned, centralized, and coordinated than it really is. Dismisses accident and chaos. Ignores misperceptions of others. Fundamental attribution error possibly caused by cultural bias.
Proportionality Bias	Expectation that the adversary will expend efforts proportionate to the ends he seeks. Interference about the intentions of others from costs and consequences of actions they initiate.
Rational-Actor Hypothesis	Assumption that others will act in a "rational" manner based on one's own rational reference. Results from ethnocentrism, mirror imaging, or ignorance.
Willful Disregard of New Evidence	Rejection of information that conflicts with already-held beliefs. Results from prior commitments, and/or excessive pursuit of consistency
Worst-Case Analysis (Cassandra Complex)	Excessive skepticism. Reflects pessimism and extreme caution, based on predilection (cognitive predisposition), adverse past experience, or on support of personal or organizational interest or policy preferences.

symptoms. Two of the fundamental characteristics of the Groupthink are the tendency of the groups to polarize and to consensualize - univocally - the members of that group towards a single common vision.

Since the groupthink is considered a syndrome, it is possible to identify some symptoms that forewarn (Paul't Hart, 1991).

Table 4. Symptoms of Groupthink according to Mintz and Wayne (2016)

TYPE	MEANING
excessive confidence in the group's abilities	a shared optimism spreads which leads to the illusion that the group is invincible and it is therefore possible, even reasonably, to take extreme risks; in addition, the decision-making group is considered to be of unmentionable morality, allowing to reject any ethical criticism made by third parties following the decisions.
characterized by the narrow-mindedness of the members	they minimize the occurrence of warnings that would lead to reconsider their choices and justify their action by trying to give a rational explanation; moreover, a stereotyped vision of the enemy is spreading among the members, which precludes consideration of alternative actions.
determined by the tendency to internal compliance within the group	the members impose themselves and impose on the comrades a censure of deviations from the consent with respect to the decision approved by the majority. In this way we reach unanimity, an illusory unanimity. To prevent contrary opinions being moved, the members put a direct pressure on those who try to expose them, thus the mindguard figure protects the group from ideas different from the shared one.

Table 5. Symptoms of Groupthink according to Mintz and Wayne (2016)

TYPE	MEANING
Invulnerability	the shared conviction about the success of a decision. Overconfidence that leads to irrational decisions. The collective belief that "we are too powerful or the best"
Rationale	Collective construction of rationalization to discredit warnings and negative feedback.
Morality	The group believes that their path is morally the right path. Thus, they don't consider the moral and ethical results of their actions. This is a war between good and evil. Hence we can do any means necessary.
Stereotypes	Stereotypical views on opponents Underestimating the enemy
Pressure	Group pressure to "domesticate dissenters". Any critical stance is downgraded and avoided. Belittling dissenters through nicknames «Here comes Mr. Stop-the-bombing!»
Self-censorship	Group members do not voice their concerns to keep the group integrity.They are also afraid of standing against the group leader
Unanimity	Illusion that everybody shares the same view when there was no dissenting opinion raised. Belief that unanimous view is the correct view. Sense of unanimity makes the group confident about their decisions. Therefore, the group does not need to check the validity of their decision
Mindguards	Certain group members act as the protector of the group leader's decision sidelining criticisms. We must be united in these dark times. Don't criticize..

A Possible Way to Avoid Groupthink (Janis, 1982): Going outside the group thinking "outside the box." One member should always play the devil's advocate. Leaders should refrain from declaring opinion at the beginning of the meeting. Multiple advocacy. No decisions are made without an open internal bargaining process.

Polythink

The leading concept of group dynamics, groupthink, offers one explanation: policy-making groups make sub-optimal decisions due to their desire for conformity and uniformity over dissent, leading to a failure to consider other relevant possibilities. But presidential advisory groups are often fragmented and divisive.

Mintz and Wayne (2016b), scrutinizes polythink, a group decision-making dynamic whereby different members in a decision-making unit espouse a plurality of opinions and divergent policy prescriptions, resulting in a disjointed decision-making process or even decision paralysis.

Polythink is the opposite of Groupthink. It means a plurality of opinions and views that leads to; deep disagreements and a conflict among group members divergent and disjointed foreign policy decision-making process. The polythink, although it is defined by characteristics opposite to those of the groupthink, can be categorized as a distortion of the decision-making process.

It is counterintuitive to think about harmony as some kind of pathology, but the effects of shared tunnel vision are disastrous. Intelligence-policy relations require a certain amount of tension to be effective. If intelligence officials are enamored of policymakers, they will be less willing to offer candid judgments that go against policy beliefs. If policymakers accept intelligence reports uncritically, their decisions may rest on shoddy logic and misperceptions (Rovner, 2011).

Table 6. Symptoms of Polythink, according to Mintz and Wayne (2016b)

Type	Meaning
Intragroup Conflict	competing viewpoints, chronic rivalry, distrust, Turf battles
Fear of Leaks	Reluctance to share information due to the fear that someone might leak critical information to media or else...
Lack of Communication	inability to establish healthy communication between governmental agencies; Reluctance to share information
Group disunity limits policy options	Military action is inherently risky; Policymakers often hesitate to use military force unless there is a strong consensus on its strategic necessity and probability of success. Decision paralysis

CASES STUDY

Groupthink and Polythink symptoms in the Cuba Missili Crisis (1962)

The first foreign policy action of the Kennedy Administration was the action of attack Cuba, called "the Bay of Pigs". It begins with information about the history of American business in Cuba.

President Fidel Castro's rise to power in 1959; and Castro's policies, including the nationalization of land and of both Cuban and American companies.

Captain Jorge Risquet of the Revolutionary Army explains that when Cuba went into partnership in socialism with the Soviet Union and began buying Soviet oil, the Cuban military soon had to take over American oil refineries in Cuba, which refused to process Soviet oil. President Dwight D. Eisenhower retaliated with a trade embargo against Cuba, and the CIA began recruiting and training Cuban exiles to overthrow Castro's administration. A U.S. plan against Cuba was set into motion, beginning with the bombing of sugar plantations. Newly elected President John F. Kennedy altered the plans, trying to mask U.S. involvement in the Bay of Pigs invasion and withdrawing American air power. As a result, the underequipped invasion was crushed, and Cuba prepared itself for further American aggression.

For the next two years, officials at the U.S. State Department and the Central Intelligence Agency (CIA) attempted to push Castro from power. Many Cubans welcomed Fidel Castro's 1959 overthrow of the dictatorial President Fulgencio Batista, yet the new order on the island just about 100 miles from the United States made American officials nervous. Batista had been a corrupt and repressive dictator, but he was considered to be pro-American and was an ally to U.S. companies.

At that time, American corporations and wealthy individuals owned almost half of Cuba's sugar plantations and the majority of its cattle ranches, mines and utilities. Batista did little to restrict their operations. He was also reliably anticommunist. Castro, by contrast, disapproved of the approach that Americans took to their business and interests in Cuba. It was time, he believed, for Cubans to assume more control of their nation. In January 1961, the U.S. government severed diplomatic relations with Cuba and stepped up its preparations for an invasion.

The Cuban missile crisis in 1962 offers and interesting study case over the relations between intelligence agencies and the state. Intelligence agencies produced a secret report discovering the possession by Cuba of medium range nuclear missiles within it's boundaries capable of reaching the territory of the US; what happened was that state institutional actors entered the decision making stage in a competing manner due to their differing opinions and interests.

The military, which could be arguably seen as biased by security anxiety and the need of international military dominance, strongly argued to launch a preventive attack on Cuba which could be carried by air striking the deposits where the Intelligence located the bombs or by a full scale invasion of the island.

The CIA argued that such a action could not be able to fully eradicate all the bombs, detected and possibly undetected ones, and could become politically costly and unsuccessful, reminiscing the disastrous "Bay of pigs" operation of the previous year.

President Kennedy in the end decided to establish and embargo and follow the "diplomatic" way, achieving the disarmament of Cuba nonviolently.

When US aircraft confirmed the presence of missiles in Cuba, President Kennedy created an ad hoc committee, the EXCOMM, the Executive Committee of the National Security Council. Within this committee, Kennedy wanted to include the - he appointed - director of the Central Intelligence Agency, John McCone. Although the latter was initially in favor of an ultimatum against the Soviets lasting twenty-four hours, after which he would have suggested proceeding with a surgical air intervention, he changed his mind once the US air force declared that it was not in able to hit all targets with one shot at a time. In particular, Kennedy relied heavily on intelligence through the figure of McCone, so much so that the latter was sent by the president directly by Eisenhower in order to investigate what could be the best strategy to pursue during the Cuban missile crisis. Kennedy was not subject to "cognitive biases" because he did not stop in front of his own idea and will but tried to collect as many opinions as possible in order to have a general overview of the gravity of the thing.

The support that the Kennedy administration has given to the invasion plan drawn up by a group of intelligence officers, ambitious and with little experience in the military sphere, with the aim of overthrowing the Castro regime is considered a perfect failure.

The government group that approved the decision was made up of some of the most brilliant men in the United States, however the assumptions underlying the support for the plan were wrong and there was a failure already in the early stages. The proposal to train Cuban exiles and then to intervene militarily was presented for the first time by Nixon and adopted under the Eisenhower administration. With the election of Kennedy the administration was informed by the CIA of these plans and took eight days to deliberate. The decision to continue to approve the operation was taken unanimously as the successes were considered probable. In reality the plan proved to be a failure, as the Americans did not support the Cuban exiles militarily, employing the navy or the aviation, given the cost that would have resulted and the aversion of public opinion. The invasion led to a strengthening of the Castro regime and led to the subsequent missile crisis, but neither Kennedy nor the government decision-making group took into consideration, or thought it could come true, such a scenario. The president was defined by the press of the time as incredulous in front of the facts and openly declared that he did not understand how such a rational government could get caught up in such reckless action; the members of the group had the same reaction.

According to Mintz theory on Cognitive Biases (2016), the military body was inappropriately action-oriented/interest biased neglecting the eventual competitor response by the USSR, possibly causing the rise of a new world war.

T. Sorensen was the special counsel President Kennedy. He outlined the possible responses to the Cuban situation that were discussed in the White House. The U.S. government instituted a blockade against all ships going to Cuba but kept the situation from the press, as Kennedy's press secretary, Pierre Salinger, explains. A clip follows of the announcement that Kennedy finally made to the American people alerting them to the missile crisis. Tensions heightened as Soviet and U.S. Navy ships faced off near Cuba, and both the American military and forces throughout the Soviet bloc and Cuba prepared for war (Sorensen, 1991).

Sorensen identified four reasons mentioned by Kennedy himself.

- The first factor concerns the pressures made by the CIA to convince Kennedy to approve the plan, leveraging on the political consequences obtainable in a Cold War perspective
- the second one refers to a new administration (the plan was proposed to Kennedy as soon as he was elected) bottled up in an old bureaucracy: the members of the administration did not forcefully expose their opinions because they were in a new dimension in which they feared to be criticized
- the third one concerns the secrecy of the operation and the impossibility of dealing with external experts at the highest levels of the State
- finally, the fourth factor is linked to the personal reputation of the members who could have suffered if they departed from a plan established by the previous administration.

The official explanation was, however, according to Janis (1983) incomplete as the symptoms of groupthink are evident within the Kennedy administration. Within the group there was the illusion of being invulnerable and the illusion of unanimity; personal doubts were suppressed through self-censorship or pressure exerted by the mindguard figure, who was represented in the Kennedy administration by Robert Kennedy; critical opinions were rejected at the start and the leader, with the approval of the leadership, was able to put pressure on the members.

In the Janis thought, the failure of the administration due to the groupthink was both in not evaluating the negative consequences and, a priori, in not considering the assumptions underlying the decision to approve the plan wrong. The desire to maintain unity in the group has led to overestimating their vulnerability and underestimating the risks, as well as a final discrepancy between expectations and reality.

Janis identifies some applicable precautions to prevent a decision-making group from falling victim to the groupthink and that the decision-making processes are ineffective. That they are actually usable is evident in the case of the Cuban missile crisis, when Kennedy, who often declared his dismay at the negative outcome of the decisions taken by a group of brilliant men, introduced new rules that proved useful. However, although we are aware of ways to avoid this syndrome, we are again faced with situations in which the decisions taken seem to stem from a fallacious decision-making process, due to the presence of groupthink within a government group. A case in point is the case of the 2003 US government's attack on Iraq. Scholars have wondered over the years whether the decision to intervene militarily depended on a failure of the rules to avoid groupthink, or an incapacity to apply them.

To understand if this is a case of groupthink, Janis identifies four questions to be answered.

- The first concerns who made the decision, whether the leader or the whole group and whether this group is cohesive; in fact, in the case of the Bush administration, he was not very skilled in foreign policy and often took his staff's suggestions into consideration.
- The second question concerns decision-making and whether it is defective; in the Bush administration there were several indications of a fallacious decision-making process: for example, the information available was poorly evaluated and processed.
- The third question that Janis proposes is whether the symptoms of groupthink are also noted in the decisions deriving from the process; the answer is also in this affirmative case since the unbridled search for a constant agreement has led to an overestimation of the group's abilities, to internal pressures to conform the members and to a closed mentality to all that was external to the group.
- The fourth and last question concerns the presence of the structural conditions that precede the decision-making process and that are necessary for the presence of the groupthink; also in this case the Bush administration presents the required characteristics, since the decision-making group was formed by a small, very cohesive elite. Given the answers to these questions it is clear that the decision to invade Iraq was taken by an administration characterized by the groupthink syndrome, however, as Janis points out, not all decisions made by a group subjected to groupthink lead to harmful outcomes and, on the contrary, not all decisions taken in the absence of groupthink lead to positive results. If these conditions had not existed, the invasion of Iraq might have been better planned, but it would probably still have been chosen as the way forward.

Groupthink and Polythink Symptoms in The US Decision to Invade Iraq in 2003

Mintz and DeRouen (2013) compare the military campaigns of Afghanistan in 2001 and Iraq in 2003, and come to the following conclusions: President Bush has applied to Iraq the same strategy used for Afghanistan (invasion by land forces) ignoring the fact that the two countries have different populations and a very different background in social, ethnic and religious terms. Similarly, when organizing the occupation phase in Iraq, the administration had in mind the post-WWII Western European model and the guaranteed support in Seoul in South Korea. But Iraq was not a "friendly area" and the Americans soon realized that the strategy adopted did not allow for the implementation of an effective counterinsurgency. The authors refer to episodes like this with the term "historical analogy bias".

To stay on the subject, the authors highlight the weight of the "poliheuristic bias": the political decision maker who suffers from it tends to avoid the choice of alternatives that could harm him politically or personally. In these terms, Bush's unwillingness to take into consideration the idea of the withdrawal of troops from Iraq should be read. Marrin's essay proposes a very interesting case study: the question of the territorial integrity of Yugoslavia lends itself to a double interpretation.

On the one hand, the 1990 the New Institutional Economics (NIE), which foresaw a violent disintegration of the federation, would not have been taken into consideration by US policymakers because they essentially contradicted their vision: a stable Yugoslavia turned out to be the most convenient scenario. At this juncture the warning would therefore have been ignored due to cognitive limits and political predisposition. We can therefore speak of Confirmation bias in Pattern-Recognition Biases group.

The decision to invade Iraq in 2003 is representative of both the case of groupthink and poly thing. The neoconservative group that constituted the presidential cabinet was incredibly united with the same vision, conceptions and they had even before the beginning of the war a policy project for what concerned Iraq and the Middle East. On the other hand at the same moment we can find what can be described as polythink firstly among different branches of the American intelligence services where there was a lack of coordination and also mistrust, which led firstly the CIA to think that the major terrorist attacks would have been outside the US.

The same happened in a certain way among the top tier decision makers where the SecDef Donald Rumsfeld fiercely disagreed with the Secretary of State Colin Powell who had always a cautious approach in foreign policy and preferred to use military interventions as an extrema ratio (indeed, he was known as the "reluctant warrior"). At the end this clash could be interpreted both as the case of the mind guard in groupthink (role played by Rumsfeld, among the Bush's inner circle of the US executive) who succeed to bring back in the right way the "black sheep", but also as polythink because the clash was extended to others branches of the American intelligence and armed forces.

In the Marrin's vision (2013), the Iraqi case clearly show us that intelligence analysis could be redundant especially if the decision makers are very experienced. Decision makers are often the same and they could have had military experience, political experience or both, especially in American politics, and they collect and gather a lot of intel during the time in which they are in charge and when they are at the opposition. This continuity in the milieu of power allowed them to shape a conception of the issue and act consequently. Iraq was a central issue in the American foreign policy in Middle East since the 80s, it was a fact that they used WMDs against civilians, and the US even fought a war against it a decade before, American decision makers had all the time to shape their vision and their idea of what should have been done in Iraq, as a consequence the new intel was redundant or irrelevant for the policy that they had already decided.

This perfectly introduce the theory of politicization described by Rovner. In *Fixing the Facts* (2013), Joshua Rovner explores the complex interaction between intelligence and policy and shines a spotlight on the problem of politicization. Major episodes in the history of American foreign policy have been closely tied to the manipulation of intelligence estimates. Rovner describes how the Johnson administration dealt with the intelligence community during the Vietnam War; how President Nixon and President Ford politicized estimates on the Soviet Union; and how pressure from the George W. Bush administration contributed to flawed intelligence on Iraq. He also compares the U.S. case with the British experience between 1998 and 2003, and demonstrates that high-profile government inquiries in both countries were fundamentally wrong about what happened before the war.

Rovner states that we know nowadays is that American decision makers and their allies had already made their decision about Iraq and they accepted only the intel that confirmed their visions and ideas. What happened in the Niger gate case is crystal clear: a manipulated dossier about the Iraqi's purchase of yellowcake uranium from Niger spread among western intelligence and contributed to create the casus belli showing that Iraq was effectively trying to build up a vast WMD arsenal. A lot of analysts in western agencies labelled that report as false and "intoxicated" but eventually it has been used by decision makers.

Looking at the definition that the author gives of indirect manipulation I believe that it is not a question of exclusion: the community intelligence certainly perceived the need for the administration of specific results in the period between 2002 and 2003 exasperating the forecasts on the worst possible scenario. The latter is typical of the period close to 9/11, as Gill and Phytian said (2012: 215) recalling the meeting at the White House in November 2001 during which Vice President Cheney is sure: << If there is a possibility of 'one percent that the Pakistani scientists are helping al Qaeda build or develop a nuclear weapon, we must consider it a certainty in terms of response (...) >>.

Groupthink and Polythink Symptoms in The First Gulf War

The Gulf War (Aug 1990 - Feb 1991) also known as the first Gulf was the conflict that opposed Iraq to a coalition of 35 states formed under the auspices of the UN and led by the United States, which sought to restore the sovereignty of the small emirate of Kuwait, after it had been invaded and annexed by Iraq.

It was the first real American military intervention from the total defeat of the war in Vietnam, sanctioned by the collapse of Saigon in 1975. The Bush administration therefore had to manage a decidedly complicated situation, since it was in the need to intervene but also had to take considering the American public opinion, strongly anti-interventionist and reluctant to intervene in another war that could have had disastrous results like the one in Vietnam. The Americans suffered from the "Vietnam syndrome": a war that in their thoughts should have ended in a couple of months but that actually kept them busy for many years and eventually there were more than 500,000 victims. In the Mintz's analysis of cognitive bias (Mintz&Wayne, 2016), especially on the concept of "stability bias", American citizens preferred to avoid what in their minds was a re-proposal of the greatest political-military defeat in their history and many believed that they did not have to intervene. Another type of bias relating to the Gulf War, in a confirmatory type, to the extent that greater attention is paid to memorable events and the factors that may conflict with one's own convictions are deliberately ignored. In reality,

George H. Bush could not avoid going to war. The solution he adopted was based on three factors:

- recognize the UN as the only entity capable of authorizing an armed conflict (the UN approved a resolution to free Kuwait in January 1991),
- the creation of a vast international coalition with the exception of Israel, in order not to create friction with the Arab countries for the first time included in the coalition,
- minimize American casualties, with the use of targeted and surgical bombardments and with the minimum use of ground troops.

Bush's three-arrow strategy proved a success and on February 24, the UN coalition rejected Iraqi troops out of Kuwait City. Speaking of the Gulf War, Marrin (2013) emphasized the reasons why the intelligence did not work. First, the intelligence was not able to provide correct and accurate information; in fact shortly before the outbreak of the war analysts were convinced that the war would not break out because the Iraqis knew of a possible retaliation from the United States and this was not a risk they were willing to run. Secondly, as Paul Wolfowitz says, policy-makers were aware of the risk of a possible war between Iraq and Kuwait and had already drawn up action plans for future US intervention, bypassing the intelligence reports they considered the war as unlikely (Davis, 2007). This last point can be linked to Rovner's theory of politicization, to the extent that policy-makers tend to maintain their position of strength in their relationship with the intelligence services and ignore them since they possess more punctual and precise information.

Groupthink and Polythink Symptoms in 9/11 Attack Management

According to Mintz and Wayne (2016), the starting point is the 9/11 commission report made in 2004 that stated that the attacks were made possible because of the communication failures between different parts of the government and security agencies. The authors state that the 9/11 attacks have a lot of symptoms that are unique to the Polythink syndrome. First of all, there were large disagreements between the most important parts of the advisory group. Secondly, there were also leaks and the fear of leaks. The information could not be given to others, because of a fear that the information would be leaked. A third reason for Polythink was the confusion and a lack of communication.

There was a lot of information but the various agencies could not share it. Furthermore, there was a lot of intragroup competition, and information was not shared. Fourth there was also a limited review of policy alternatives, objectives, risks, and contingencies. The fifth reason for the Polythink syndrome was the failure to reappraise previously rejected alternatives. Because it is so hard to make a decision, decisions did not get revised afterwards even if they were not very good. The sixth reason for the Polythink syndrome were the framing effects and the selective use of information. The last two symptoms are the lowest-commondenominator decisions and decision paralysis.

The chapter concludes by saying that the 9/11 attacks had some Groupthink features, for example, the high level from external threats and the illusion that they would not attack the U.S. Why this is a good example was explained previously by the symptoms.

Anyway, this was one of the most obvious facilitators of Polythink. The political concerns were very high at 9/11, security decisions are most of the time not popular with the electorate. Next to political concerns, there were also normative differences, the national behavior is according to the authors a sum of beliefs of actors, which can differ from each other. The experts and novices had a different way of decision-making. Military personnel was against a military action while the civilian advisors were pro a military action.

LABORATORY

The Case of Pattern-Recognition Biases

Introduction

Imagine being an alien and coming to earth during a good soccer game. It is very likely that you will understand little, but with a little more observation you would understand something. If the aliens work like us humans, after repeated observations they could come to understand the basic rules of the game. They will never understand the "out of the game" but certainly the essential things, because this is what our brains do all day long, looking for patterns and patterns.

How much would the alien really understand? Let us imagine that the alien, however, due to his (her) cognitive conformation, can bear the sight of only one by time. It is likely that looking at a game that started in the second half, you will be completely blown away. As you know there is a change of field and the doors are reversed. We often do so, we look only at the first half of the game and from that, we think we have understood everything. This is just one of the biases but it clearly shows how it works.

Try to think of an example in the real life, applying ***The 6 Thinking Hats Method***. This method was created by Edward de Bono, a psychologist and doctor who specialized in cognitive scienc. He developed this new way of communicating in his book which was first published in 1985: "6 Hats to Think". It is a Method that gets the Team Working Together to Adopt all Modes of Thought.

How was this creative thinking technique born? From an observation: we are living in a society where presenting an argument can take up a large amount of room in communication. The consequence: each person presents their argument, stating their own point of view with their own sensitivity. Some people are interested in the facts, while others use their emotions to communicate. In the same way, some people are too optimistic in what they have to say, while others are excessively cautious. Finally, most of the time, discussions which involve putting down other people's ideas, can be detrimental to sharing process.

Edward de Bono suggested trying a new way of thinking within group called lateral thinking (or parallel thinking) which asks individuals to focus together on a single point of view. Using the 6 Thinking Hats method a team can think about a situation or subject together, covering all points of view, in the same way, at the same time.

Table 7. Six Thinking Hats

TYPE OF HAT (COLOR)	MEANING
White	The Facts. With the white hat, a team only formulate ideas with the facts and no comments or interpretations.
Green	Creativity and New Ideas. With the green hat, team members are free to make any proposals which come to mind
Black	The Risks and Weaknesses of an Idea. The black hat provides team members with the opportunity to think and give ideas in the most pessimistic way possible
Yellow	Hopes and Advantages. The team takes up a firm positive position.
Red	Emotions. With the red hat, the team expresses its feelings, whatever they are, without the need to justify them.
Blue	Control and organization. The blue hat is special as it guides all the others. It symbolizes taking a step back and organizing the discussions. When the team thinks with the blue hat, they propose solutions and organise how they are put into effect.

The Rules of this Collaborative Game. The principle of the 6 Thinking Hats is simple: each hat corresponds to a position, which all the team members must adopt at the same time.

Assignment. Analyze the following Problematic Situation: a Mafia repentant speaks of a possible attack on Republic Day. Discover the 6 existing colors with their meaning and see a concrete illustrationn of the ideas that may be generated, according to *Six Thinking Hats*. Note that the hat is a position and never corresponds to a person, but a vision, a point of view. This means that the exercise requires all the team members to adopt the same hat (the same position) at the same time. As the discussions progress, the team changes hats until they've looked at all aspects that need to be examined.

REFERENCES

Davis, J. (2007). *Paul Wolfowitz on Intelligence Policy-Relations.* The Challenge of Managing Uncertainty. Retrieved from https://www.cia.gov/library/center-for-the-study-of-intelligence/csi-publications/csi-studies/studies/96unclass/davis.htm

DeBono, E. (1985). *Six Thinking Hats: An Essential Approach to Business Management.* Little, Brown, and Company.

Galinsky, A., & Moskowitz, G. (2000). Perspective-taking: Decreasing stereotype expression, stereotype accessibility, and in-group favoritism. *Journal of Personality and Social Psychology, 78*(4), 702–724. doi:10.1037/0022-3514.78.4.708 PMID:10794375

Gill, P., & Phytian, M. (2012). *Intelligence in an Insecure World.* Polity.

Janis, I. L. (1983). *Groupthink: Psychological studies of policy decisions and fiascoes.* Boston, MA: Houghton Mifflin.

Jonas, E., Schulz-Hardt, S., Frey, D., & Thelen, N. (2001). Confirmation bias in sequential information search after preliminary decisions: An expansion of dissonance theoretical research on selective exposure to information. *Journal of Personality and Social Psychology, 80*(4), 557–571. doi:10.1037/0022-3514.80.4.557 PMID:11316221

Kahneman, D. (2002). Maps of bounded rationality: a perspective on intuitive judgment and choice. Prize Lecture, December 8. Princeton University, Department of Psychology, Princeton, NJ.

Kahneman, D., Fredrickson, D. L., Schreiber, C. A., & Redelmeier, D. A. (1993). When more pain is preferred to less: Adding a better end. *Psychological Science, 4*(6), 401–405. doi:10.1111/j.1467-9280.1993.tb00589.x

Krizan, L. (1999). *Intelligence Essential for Everyone*. Washington, DC: Joint Military Intelligence College, June 1999. Retrieved from: NATO Open Source Intelligence Handbook, http://www.au.af.mil/au/awc/awcgate/nato/osint_hdbk.pdf

Marrin, S. (2013). Revisiting Intelligence and Policy: Problems with Politicization and Receptivity. In Intelligence and National Security. Routledge.

Mintz, A., & DeRouen, K. (2010). *Understanding Foreign Policy Decision Making*. Cambridge University Press. doi:10.1017/CBO9780511757761

Mintz, A., & Wayne, C. (2016). The Polythink Syndrome: U.S. Foreign Policy Decisions on 9/11, Afghanistan, Iraq, Iran, Syria, and ISIS. Stanford University Press.

Myers, D. G. (2002). *Intuition: Its powers and perils*. New Haven, CT: Yale University Press.

Paul't, H. (1991). Irving L. Janis' Victims of Groupthink. *Political Psychology, 12*(2), 247–278. doi:10.2307/3791464

Payne, K. (2005). Conceptualizing control in social cognition: How executive functioning modulates the expression of automatic stereotyping. *Journal of Personality and Social Psychology, 89*(4), 488–503. doi:10.1037/0022-3514.89.4.488 PMID:16287413

Reinhard, M.-A., Greifeneder, R., & Scharmach, M. (2013). nconscious processes improve lie detection. *Journal of Personality and Social Psychology, 105*(5), 721–739. doi:10.1037/a0034352 PMID:24219784

Richards, J. (1999). Psychology of Intelligence Analysis, Center for the Study of Intelligence. Central Intelligence Agency, Part III - Cognitive Biases, 111-172.

Rovner J. (2011). *Fixing the Facts: National Security and the Politics of Intelligence*. Cornell University Press.

Sorensen. (1991). Introduction. In J. *F. Kennedy 'Let the Word Go Forth': The Speeches, Statements, and Writings of John F. Kennedy, 1947–1963* (Reprint ed.). New York: Laurel.

Stanovich, K. E., & West, R. F. (2000). Individual differences in reasoning: Implications for the rationality debate. *Behavioral and Brain Sciences*, *23*(5), 645–665. doi:10.1017/S0140525X00003435 PMID:11301544

Strick, M., Stoeckart, P. F., & Dijksterhuis, A. (2015). Thinking in Black and White: Conscious thought increases racially biased judgments through biased face memory. *Consciousness and Cognition*, *36*, 206–218. doi:10.1016/j.concog.2015.07.001 PMID:26164254

Tversky, A., & Kahneman, D. (1981). The framing of decisions and the psychology of choice. *Science*, *211*(4481), 453–458. doi:10.1126cience.7455683 PMID:7455683

KEY TERMS AND DEFINITIONS

6 Thinking Hats Method: It is a good decision-making technique and method for group discussions and individual thinking. Combined with the parallel thinking process, this technique helps groups think more effectively. It is a means to organize thinking processes in a detailed and cohesive manner.

Cognitive Bias: It is a systematic pattern of deviation from the norm or from rationality in judgment. The bias is a form of distortion of the evaluation caused by the injury. A person's mind map presents bias where it is conditioned by pre-existing concepts not necessarily connected to one another by logical and validities.

Cognitive Science: It studies the mind, and as discipline, involves the scientific interchange among researchers in various areas of study, including artificial intelligence, linguistics, anthropology, psychology, neuroscience, philosophy, and education.

Groupthink: The term indicates a way of thinking that people adopt when they are deeply involved in a highly cohesive group, where the tendency to reach unanimity prevails over the motivation to realistically evaluate more functional alternatives for action (Janis, 1982, p. 9).

Polythink: It is a group decision-making dynamic whereby different members in a decision-making unit espouse a plurality of opinions and divergent policy prescriptions, resulting in a disjointed decision-making process or even decision paralysis.

Chapter 3
Policy Making, Crisis Management, and Leadership Intelligence:
A New Framework of Analysis

ABSTRACT

Leadership analysts support policymakers by producing and delivering written and oral assessments of foreign leaders and key decision-makers. This chapter explores how the foreign policy of a state is strongly influenced by the personality of the president and the type of government in office. Some case studies are referred and analyzed, such as the Gulf War of 1991. The authors apply a new framework of analysis, called Orientism Management (OM), that proposes 10 different knowledge management types.

INTRODUCTION

Leadership Analysts support policymakers by producing and delivering assessments of foreign leaders and key decision-makers, by examining their worldviews, national ambitions and constraints, and the social context of these leaders.

Sometimes, counterparts can quickly change, showing significant differences among leaders of the same country. For example, in the case of the USA, ideologies, beliefs, and inclinations of the last three Presidents have

DOI: 10.4018/978-1-7998-1562-4.ch003

been totally different, both in domestic and foreign politics. The approach that Bush had towards the Muslim world, influenced by the events of September 11, was one of distrust and prevention with those who could have relations with Al Qaeda. It was an obvious aggressive foreign policy, legitimized as defensive. Instead, Obama has activated a more pacifist policy, aimed at promoting good relations with the Muslim world, also taking into account the presence of a heterogeneous electorate in the USA, mostly Muslim. As for Trump, his foreign policy appears, in some respects, unpredictable, without compromise. Even his strong, direct and little diplomatic language proves it, and at times many media have called him provocative at the international level.

This type of analysts comes from the fields of social psychology and political science and takes a quantitative methodology when conducting analysis. In addition, they can explore quantitative measures such as verbal styles, grammatical choices, and scales for achievement, affiliation, and power provide room for analysis.

Table 1. Traditional sectors of analysis

SECTOR	DESCRIPTION
Cultural and historical background	Constraints of the political culture on the role of the leader
Personality	1. General personal description (Appearance and personal characteristics, Health) 2. Intellectual capacity and style (Intelligence, Judgment, Knowledge, Cognitive complexity 3. Emotional reactions (Moods, mood variability; Impulse and impulse control) 4. Drives and character structure (Personality types; Psychodynamics; Conscience and scruples; Psychological drives, needs, motives; Motivation for seeking leadership role) 5. Interpersonal relationships (Key relationships and characterize nature of relationships)
Worldview	1. Perceptions of political reality (include cultural influences/biases) 2. Core beliefs (include concept of leadership, power) 3. Political philosophy, ideology, goals, and policy views (domestic, foreign, and economic policy views) 4. Nationalism and identification with country
Leadership System	1. General characteristics (the leader's political and cultural determinants and skill in fulfilling them) 2. Strategy and tactics- goal-directed behavior 3. Decision making and decision implementation style (Strategic decision making; Crisis decision making; Dealing with formal and informal negotiating style)

A prerequisite in the cultural background of the Political Leader is to own or practice a design culture, to give concrete and coherent implementation to innovative and effective logic.

Table 2. The most famous Leadership Styles

STYLE	DESCRIPTION
Democratic Leadership	the leader makes decisions based on the input of each team member. This type is one of the most effective leadership styles because it allows lower-level collaborators to exercise the authority they'll need to use wisely in future positions they might hold.
Autocratic Leadership	In this leadership style, the leader makes decisions without taking input from anyone who reports to them. The consequences of this approach clearly are to lose collaborators or not to consider crucial support by them.
Laissez-Faire Leadership	It is the least intrusive form of leadership. It can empower collaborators by trusting them to work however they'd like, but it can also limit their development and overlook success opportunities.
Strategic Leadership	Strategic leaders accept the burden of executive interests while ensuring that current working conditions remain stable for everyone else and supporting multiple types of collaborators at once.
Transformational Leadership	Collaborators might have a basic set of tasks and goals, but the leader constantly encourages them outside of their scheduling, to get better performance in unpredictability conditions.
Transactional Leadership	The leaders reward their collaborators for precisely the work they do. Transactional leadership helps establish roles and responsibilities for each collaborator, but it can also encourage bare-minimum work if collaborators know how much their effort is worth all the time.
Coach-Style Leadership	this leader focuses on identifying and nurturing the individual strengths of each member on the team and also focuses on strategies that will enable their team to work better together.
Bureaucratic Leadership	This style of leadership might listen and consider the input of collaborators, unlike autocratic leadership, but the leader tends to reject a collaborator's input if it conflicts with own worldview policy or past practices.

Topics of Discussion

The following discussion points come from information in this chapter:

How does leader use staff/inner circle? Does the leader vet decisions or use them only for information? How collegial? Does the leader surround himself or herself with sycophants or choose strong self-confident subordinates? Especially, a Leadership Analyst should predict how the individual will interact with other political figures, including opposition leaders and other key foreign leaders in crisis situations.

ORIENTISM MANAGEMENT FRAMEWORK

The present study refers to the Orientism Management (OM) concept (dall'Acqua&Md Santo, 2014) to describe Leaders' risk management. OM is a new knowledge management approach, scientifically based on:

- HSB-KM Human System Biology-based KM model framework (Md Santo, 2013) about the definition of Nature and Human Knowledgeto design a semantic interpretation of the knowledge process
- DHE Design Human Engineering (Bandler et al, 2013) about the definition of criteria to improve the people's ability of contextual changesto design political strategies to apply

OM principle considers a political ecosystem as a community of people in conjunction with different societal/political environment, interacting as a system. These components are regarded as linked together through knowledge cycles and energy flows (pathways).

The framework dedicates attention to different "plans" in the decision-making process:

- **Prescriptive Plan:** how political leaders should reason
- **Descriptive Plan:** how they reason
- **Social Plan:** what type of reasoning motivates the decisional action in terms of efficacy and efficiency
- **Communicative Plan:** what type of reasoning is recognizable
- **Management Plan:** what conditions guarantee "order" in a process, against networking, understanding, and learning "chaos"
- **Tutoring Plan:** how political leaders can be supported in their choosing process
- **Historic Plan:** how a diachronic vision (history) of the issues and own previous experiences can lead decisions
- **Comparative Plan:** how a synchronic vision (comparing transversal situations and conditions) can lead decisions
- **Creative Plan:** how to innovate
- **Simulation Plan:** how to simulate cases study

Leadership Mindset

Key points of Orientism concept are (dall'Acqua, 2019):

- the creation of new models of behavior
- the simultaneity of how we process information
- larger pieces of human experience are to be put together to achieve success
- the complex interconnection between reference points

New variables, factors, and criteria are needed to direct and motivate the mind in the decisional process, in self-reference, to be considered in a lifelong guidance to have success in choices, assumptions of responsibilities and achievement of objectives, over the uncertainty.

OM is composed by intertwined 10 Knowledge Management (KM) typologies, each based on areas of development and improvement of own personal leadership: KM with consciousness (3 levels), meaning, feeling, will, understanding, personalization, availability, synergy.

Figure 1. KMs of OM Strategy

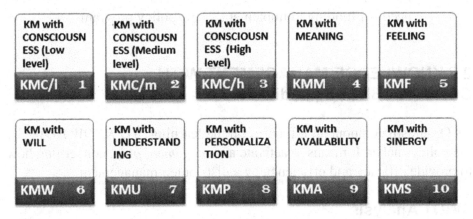

The outcome is the design of a training strategy for Political Leaders, and a possible grid of analysis.

1ST KNOWLEDGE MANAGEMENT WITH CONSCIOUSNESS (low level) - KMC/l

As Orientism's component, it focuses on the learning *"TO KNOW WHAT"* by the Political Leader. It means to activate a *prescriptive plan*, that concerns a knowledge base of an updated regulatory guide, according to own school profile, educational needs, and a possible offer.

SWOT Analysis

- *Strenght points*
  - ○ Professional identity training
- *Weakness points*
  - ○ Complexity of the political system, national/international society
  - ○ Deep change in the management needs
- *Opportunities*
  - ○ Political Leader as a crucial agent of the domestic, foreign, and economic policy
  - ○ Getting better remuneration in the role
- *Threads*
  - ○ normative legislation and/or contradictory political debate in Parliament
  - ○ needs of funding to implement a new policy program

2ND KNOWLEDGE MANAGEMENT WITH CONSCIOUSNESS (medium level) - KMC/M

As Orientism component, it focuses on the learning *"TO KNOW HOW"* by the policy-maker. It means to activate a *management plan*, concerning how to provide efficacy and efficiency by a distributed management.

SWOT Analysis

- *Strength points*
  - ○ needs of leadership paradigm change
- *Weakness points*
  - ○ multiplicity of responsibilities
  - ○ mistakes of leadership
  - ○ collaborators coordination in relation to the process of change
- *Opportunities*
  - ○ middle management
  - ○ Intelligence Agencies

- *Threads*
  - low or not adequate human resources

3RD KNOWLEDGE MANAGEMENT WITH CONSCIOUSNESS (high level) - KMC/H

As Orientism component, it focuses on the learning *"TO KNOW WHERE"* by thePolicy-maker It means to activate a *descriptive plan*, concerning contextualizeddesign and action.

SWOT Analysis

- *Strenght points*
  - to can control the management process as "action pin". An *Action Pin* is used to define the data values passed out of and into an Action. An *input pin* provides values to the Action, whereas an *output pin* contains the results from that Action.
  - Knowledge of the territory and its resources also for guidance activities
- *Weakness points*
  - Work on multiple sides
- *Opportunities*
  - fundings
  - top down a bottom-up support
- *Threads*
  - to identify critical contextualized relationships between Political Leader and other stakeholders.

4TH KNOWLEDGE MANAGEMENT WITH MEANING - KMM

As Orientism's component, it focuses on the learning *"TO KNOW WHY"*, that the Political Leader needs to manage. It means to activate a *social plan*, concerning a reasonable motivation for decisional actions in terms of efficacy and efficiency.

SWOT Analysis

- *Strenght points*
  - ○ solid regulatory system
- *Weakness points*
  - ○ Lack trust and conviction in the current political system and law
- *Opportunities*
  - ○ Professional Upgrade Courses
- *Threads*
  - ○ Hostile Parliament
  - ○ Hostile political staff

5ᵀᴴ KNOWLEDGE MANAGEMENT WITH FEELING (KMF)

As Orientism's component, it focuses on the learning *"TO KNOW MOVING (TOWARDS)"*, byPolitical Leader to activate a change of perspective or action. It means to activate a general personalized *tutoringplan*, concerning how to support Political Leaders in their personal choosing process.

SWOT Analysis

- *Strenght points*
  - ○ emotional intelligence
- *Weakness points*
  - ○ difficulty to manage stress
  - ○ weak attitude with subordinates
- *Opportunities*
  - ○ balanced human resource support
- *Threads*
  - ○ strong hostility between Parliament members or with other foreign Political Leaders

In operational meaning, emotional intelligence is a set of soft skill for a Political Leader. It consists in:

- ***Personal Emotional intelligence*** is the ability to manage oneself, own inner environment, autonomy, self-critique, assumption of responsibility (*internal ecology*)
- ***Social-Emotional intelligence*** is the ability to manage relationships, the external social environment (*external ecology*)

Table 3. Intelligence ecology

Type	characteristic	Main behavioral features
Internal	Governing Personal Emotional intelligence can support Political Leader to understand the circumstances and causes that trigger them.	***Self-mastery or self-control***: a. Knowledge how to handle anxiety and emotions in a reasonable and profitable manner even under stress, learning to temper reactions; b. Attitude of tolerance and understanding of opinions other than theirs (interest in understanding them)
		From egocentrism to social self: a.Availability to listen and understand the other (active listening), to identify oneself with the other (empathy, tuning), to appreciate the contribution of others, enhancing them; b. Knowledge how to think as a community, as well as individuality
		Inner strength:a. Self-esteem, but not arrogance, b. Capacity and availability for self-learning, c. Assertiveness (affirmation of self and ideas in constructive terms), d. Enthusiasm (the pleasure of working and solving problems), e. Self-motivation, overcoming difficulties
		Voltage to the result: Mental orientation towards the production of concrete results and solutions, together with othersProfessional discipline)
External	Governing Social Emotional intelligence can support Political Leader to relate positively to others and to interact constructively with them	***Understanding the other:*** Interpersonal communication skills in public speaking (verbal and para-verbal)
		Authority and leadership: a. Ability to influence others' behavior by making them useful to the organization and to task; b. Knowledge how to manage with authority and flexibility rather than by virtue of the authority conferred; c. Actively act as Coach of your team of coadjutor, co-workers, and subordinates; d. Knowledge how to motivate your collaborators, to delegate when appropriate, possible and without prejudice to security; to decide to risk, under calculated risk conditions
		Pushing to continuous improvement: a. Attitude to solving problems rather than looking for faults; b. Monitoring the progress of projects, studies, interventions and capitalize on acquired know-how; c. Attitude to support innovative ideas and improvement; d. Knowledge how to promote lifelong learning, self-learning; e. Skills immediate positive and, if necessary, negative feedback on the performance
		Driven by the Institution's result and image: a. Knowledge how to dress up the institutional roles (manager, member of a group, public representative of an institution, institutional leader, spontaneous, subordinate, participating in a working group etc.); b. Knowledge how to get the same from your co-workers and coadjutors; c. Ability to promote the image of the institution both inside and outside; d. Availability to offer the best of your skills and commitment

Successful Political Leaders are team-builders. They understand the importance of relationships, empower their staff and political voters and show great empathy.

6TH KNOWLEDGE MANAGEMENT WITH WILL (KMW)

As Orientism's component, it focuses on the learning *"TO KNOW EXPERIENCING"*, a process that thePolitical Leaderneeds to activate and control. It means both *historical, comparative* and *simulation plans,* about analyzing, using own, and other's previous experiences, comparing transversal situations and conditions, to make decisions, using also virtual simulation tools.

SWOT Analysis

- *Strenght points*
  - ○ scientific analysis of the decision process
- *Weakness points*
  - ○ mistakes of leadership
  - ○ not adequate or not updated competences
- *Opportunities*
  - ○ tools for reflecting activities or repository or decision simulation
  - ○ sharing of ideas between peer
- *Threads*
  - ○ low or not adequate human resources

7TH KNOWLEDGE MANAGEMENT WITH UNDERSTANDING (KMU)

As Orientism's component, it focuses on the learning *"TO KNOW ENABLING"*, that the Political Leader needs to improve. It means to activate *tutoring*, as well *management* and *socialplan*s.

SWOT Analysis

- *Strenght points*
  - ○ Sharing project and organizational design guidelines by verifying their financial compatibility
  - ○ Acquisition of information on the organizing work and security system from Intelligence Agencies
- *Weakness points*
  - ○ Progressive reduction of support activity
  - ○ Difficulty in immediate intervention
  - ○ Lack of timely responses
- *Opportunities*
  - ○ Comparison between peers (Political Leaders) of existing issues and regulatory clarifications
  - ○ Use of regional expertise to solve internal issues
  - ○ Possibility of establishing partnerships, protocols of understanding, partnerships with private and public associations
  - ○ Quality controls as feedback to be analyzed
- *Threads*
  - ○ Too much commitment to Political Leader involves high risk of errors

8TH KNOWLEDGE MANAGEMENT WITH PERSONALIZATION (KMP)

As Orientism's component, it focuses on the learning *"TO KNOW CHANGING"* by the Political Leader. It means to activate a *creating plan* to improve new dynamics, relations, and balance.

SWOT Analysis

- *Strenght points*
  - ○ Personal coordination with regard to the process of change
- *Weakness points*
  - ○ Fear of changing the legal pre-stablished order
  - ○ Tendency to individualism
- *Opportunities*

- ◦ Research new relationships with the work environment
- *Threads*
  - ◦ Resistance to reform by Parliament members

9TH KNOWLEDGE MANAGEMENT WITH AVAILABILITY (KMA)

As Orientism's component, it focuses on the learning *"TO KNOW OPENING"* towards people, environment, future and perspectives, interpretations by the Political Leader. It's part of both *creative* and *social plans*, already described.

SWOT Analysis

- *Strenght points*
  - ◦ Vertical political program: continuity of previous political strategies
- *Weakness points*
  - ◦ Not in-depth knowledge of other organizational point of view
- *Opportunities*
  - ◦ Experimenting with cross-design projects on different stakeholders by exploiting the different experiences and professionalism in the different sectors
  - ◦ Opening and dialogue with peers
- *Threads*
  - ◦ the interest to continue previous methods and strategies in a vertical political program may lose the specificity of ia leadership

10TH KNOWLEDGE MANAGEMENT WITH SYNERGY (KMS)

As Orientism's component, it focuses on the learning *"TO KNOW DEVOTING"* towards work, goals, relationships by the Political Leader. It's on the base of *all plans*, specifically, it's part of a *social plan*.

SWOT Analysis

- *Strenght points*
  - Resistance to a very complex job for passion and strong vision of own administration
- *Weakness points*
  - No tuning with the Parliament
- *Opportunities*
  - Financial and operational tools by Government to be able to accomplish innovation
- *Threads*
  - Too fast changes in legislation, sometimes contradictory

POLITICAL LEADERSHIP'S POSSIBLE MISTAKES

In synthesis, the Political Leader can fall in the following common behavioral mistakes:

- *Connected with the level of maturity of the staff*
  - To assume a style too much *directive,* risking to become *authoritarian*
  - To assume a style too much *supporting,* risking to become *paternalistic*
  - To assume a style too much *persuasive,* risking to become *handling*
  - To assume a style too much *participative,* risking *paralysis* in the relationship
  - To assume a style too much *delegating,* risking to assume an attitude of *"passing the buck"*
- *Connected with the public image or perception of the Political Leader*
  - Perceiving a *self-centric leader,* rather than coadjutor's centric relationship and their organizational growth; or a *failed leader* (laxism).
  - On the other hand, *not* perceiving *level evolution signals* in coadjutors or signs of inadequacy of an assigned role
- *Connected with the judgment of people*
  - Collaborators, always classified into two categories: motivated and reliable or lazy, irresponsible, incapable; competent (left in peace) or incompetent (always checked)

- ○ Collaborators, always classified equal, at medium level, causing not sufficiently understanding or minor management of crucial situations (between motivational support and professional reinforcement)
- **Connected with the Political Leader attitude**
  - ○ With tension "to run the game", for needs to feel "indispensable", and, usually with a very specialized vision of the school and no graduation in the assignment of tasks
  - ○ Feeling the need to get rid of the coaching role, with the consequent risks of overloading the available collaborative collaborator, or too early delegating on, and leaving alone the coadjutor, without guidance, resulting in loss of control
  - ○ With high expectations of results, leaving crucial situations in the hands of people who are not adequately competent but available, and the possible consequent disappointment or damages without forecasting

Distributed Leadership: Middle Management

The need of circulation of information top down and bottom up, and connection by all staff members makes the "coadjutors" not simply "collaborators" of the Political Leader: they support the executive management in various ways and are the "middle management". To apply this organization, Political Leaders have to manage a strategic use of delegation (supposing sufficient incomes for their additional workload, besides teaching).

This means several main possible critical factors of management, such as absence of right candidates, or leadership mistakes.

To analyze the problem, this study refers to a few historical leadership theories, evaluated among the most suitable theories: Situational Leadership of Hersey and Blanchard (1982) and Formative / Supporting Leadership of Black and Moudon(1994). Specifically, we describe the two main opposite situation:

- **Case 1: Unqualified Person:** Often a Leader has not the choice to delegate duties. If coadjutors are unqualified persons for the required role, so they need precise instructions on the job to be performed, and specific knowledge of legislation and procedures. The leader takes on the directive role of *"telling leader"*, who makes decisions for the coadjutors, plans and organizes their work.

- **Case 2: Available Person, but not yet Competent:** It's the case of a person, willing to professional development, to take responsibility, but not yet able to do the assigned work. The Leader takes on the role of "*coaching leader*", who has the responsibility of the decisions, but explains and motivates them, with the aim of actively involving the collaborator. It makes the relational level high.

- **Case 3: Competent but Insecure Person:** It's the case of a competent coadjutor, but uncertain for fear of liability, non-inclusion in the context, or no sense of belonging. The Leader takes on the role of "*empowering leader*", who is participative, decides together with the collaborator the decisions be taken to facilitate the work of the coadjutor. The relational level is high, in support, reassurance, empowerment, trust.

- **Case 4: Available, Competent, Responsible, Reliable, Self-Confident Person:** It's the case of an autonomous coadjutor, able to set goals, following the Political Leader's guidelines. The Leader takes on the role of "*delegating leader*", who defines the general reference work-guidelines, communicates the willingness to be of help and support, supervises and controls the results (not the process).

A CASE OF INDIVIDUAL LEADERSHIP LEVEL: BUSH INTERVENTION IN THE GULF WAR (1991)

J. Monten and A. Bennett (2010) studied the decision-making process during a crisis phase, specifically the American intervention in Kuwait in 1991, focusing on American leadership and the dynamics it creates. The 1991 Persian Gulf War is a "most likely" case for several crisis decision-making models. It arose during the post-Cold War budgets and involved the U.S. Army, Navy, Air Force, and Marines. The scholars put into evidence three possible paradigms of analysis.

Model 1: **The domain of the President**. It represents the situation in which, in the face of vital interests at stake, the President manages to harmonize the decision-making process by uniforming it to his will, working a particular domain in the initial phase of choice of options, that then diminishes in the implementation phase. Presidents follow personal diplomatic initiatives and makes strong public statements. Other bureaucracies are aligned with their will, and support their positions. For example, in the case of Bush policy, the

Scholars recognize this point of view in the phase prior to the intervention, the more diplomatic one, in which the role of the leader was predominant.

Model 2: **Bureaucratic policy**. The actions are the result of negotiations and compromises in which the bureaucrats defend their own interests, with a centric perspective around Administrators. The situation is exacerbated in times of crisis. This model explains how certain choices are often proposed as demanded by the context. It concerns the set agenda, with a greater balance between the three models, even if the domination of the president Bush appears to be central as foreseen by the model in the decision-making phase. The bureaucratic policy showed that both Cheney and Scowcroft support an offensive option in line with the President, but also how Baker supported a more diplomatic approach; Powell and Schwarzkopf proposed the use of force only in case of certainty of success. The organizational culture intervened when the general of the aviation McPeak proposed the use of the air force before the offensive of land, blocked by Powell that carried on a post-Vietnam culture.

Model 3: **Organizational cultures.** The focus is on the organization and on its characteristic traits as well as on the underlying culture, which prevails over decisions and power relationships. The organization acts as it is the only possible resolver of the crisis. Even in crises organizational cultures strongly shape tactical military decisions, choices among weapons systems, and the willingness of officials to risk their careers on behalf of their organizations' values. It means, for example, the decision to go to war, that still showed an active role of Bush supporting Baker's diplomatic proposal, elaborating a strategy with the Congress and giving orders to use military force. At this stage, the most interesting element is the conflict between the bureaucratic and organizational model around Powell's figure: a conflict that emerges from the discrepancy between a bureaucratic order from the superior (the president) and loyalty to his own organization. The situation was even more critical as far as Schwarzkopf was concerned, who, unlike Powell, takes a stand against the public intervention even at the cost of risking his career.

In the first political approach, however, the other models emerge: i.e. Powell and Schwarzkopf were influenced by a post-Vietnam organizational culture, according to which the intervention should be perpetrated only if, in general, they were sure of success in quick terms so as not to repeat the same mistakes; similarly, the frictions that emerge between Powell (contrary to an ambitious mission) and Cheney (supporter of the use of force) are well interpreted through the model of bureaucratic policies.

CONCLUSION

The present study offers an insight into the process of policymaking, especially with respect to handling risks in the International context of crisis. This analysis provides details on the skills that a leader in politics or high-level business management needs. Authors apply a new framework, called Orientism Management (OM), to analyze the leadership phenomenon and the main leadership profiles and characteristics. This model explores how Leadership Analysts can support policymakers by producing and delivering assessments of foreign leaders and key decision-makers. Some cases of study are referred to and analyzed.

The chapter then ends with a more detailed discussion of the specific elements of the Orientism Framework and mindset. This analysis provides a clear example of the type of powerful and well-thought-out procedures that could be brought to bear on Leadership analysis. It is an attempt to develop a leadership model which provides a strong basis for the researchers to implement the same that has been evolved from the theories in hand.

REFERENCES

Bandler, R., Roberti, A., & Fitzpatrick, O. (2013). *An Introduction To Nlp*. HarperCollins Publishers.

Monten, J., & Bennett, A. (2010). Models of Crisis Decision Making and the 1990–91 Gulf War. *Security Studies*, *19*(3), 486–520. doi:10.1080/096 36412.2010.505129

Black & Moudon. (1994). *The Managerial Grid*. Gulf Publishing.

dall'Acqua, L. (2019). Forecasting and managing risk in the health and safety sectors. Hershey, PA: IGI Global Publisher.

dall'Acqua, L., & Santo, M. (2014). Orientism, the basic pedagogical approach of PENTHA ID Model vs. 2, to manage decisions in unpredictability conditions. *Proceedings of World Congress on Engineering and Computer Science WCECS2014*, 316-21.

Hersey, P., & Blanchard, K. (1982). *Management and organizational behavior: Utilizing human resources* (4th ed.). Englewood Cliffs, NJ: Prentice-Hall.

Mitchell, D. (2005). Centralizing advisory systems: Presidential influence and the U.S. foreign policy decision-making process. *Foreign Policy Analysis*, *1*(2), 181–206. doi:10.1111/j.1743-8594.2005.00009.x

Santo, Md. (2013). *Bagaimana Knowledge Management bersama Fisika membangun* [Nature Knowledge Theory]. In 3rd Annual Forum Center for Science and Technology Development Studies – Indonesian Institute of Sciences (IPTEKIN - LIPI), Jakarta, Indonesia.

KEY TERMS AND DEFINITIONS

Intelligence Analysis: It is the process by which the information collected about an enemy is used to answer tactical questions about current operations or to predict future behavior.

Leadership Analysis (Political Sector): It support policymakers by producing and delivering assessments of foreign leaders and key decision-makers, by examining their worldviews, national ambitions and constraints, and the social context of these leaders.

Orientism Management (OM) Framework: A new multi-dimensional KM approach to improve the people's ability to manage decisions and own change of perspectives, according to natural, social, artificial environments, in personalized multi-user dynamic, assigned value to multiple reference points and multi-interpreting paradigms.

Chapter 4
Intelligence Analysis, Uncertainty, and Risk Analysis

ABSTRACT

Today we live with new threats, for the end of traditional military threats (territory and national sovereignty), the complexity of economic and commercial relations, and because the defense became "global" and implemented through information actions. Examples of new threats are telematic terrorism, international terrorism, religious fanaticism, toxic waste disposal, trafficking of sex, illegal people trafficking, and as an extension, organized crime, eversion, national economic security. Examples of new wars are cultural wars, bacteriological wars, technological wars. The chapter analyzed the concept of threat vs. risk, focusing on possible risks identification criteria and the main analytical approaches for risk management.

TOPICS FOR DISCUSSION

- In the political decision-making process, how is it possible to better organize knowledge for predictive purposes, in a field that has often be regarded as an "art" more than a "science"?
- What are the key indicators of political risks?
- What is the role of the Intelligence Analysis support in a risk management process?

DOI: 10.4018/978-1-7998-1562-4.ch004

INTRODUCTION

Since different regimes seem to pose different challenges for foreign actors, looking at political risk through this lens might help develop tools capable of more reliable and refined assessments.

In this book, Authors define different interpretations of the term "risk", according to the contexts of application and *Ex Ante Evaluation support* (see chapter 1):

- **Decision-making Under Risk:** It generally concerns risky conditions to make a decision
- **Decisional Risk:** It is connected with the difficult decision-making in itself, as a rational/cognitive process of a decision-maker.
- **Risk of a Decision:** Risk is defined as the answer to three questions: 1. What can happen? (i.e. what can go wrong?) 2. How likely is that it will happen? 3. If it does happen, what are the consequences?'
- **Risk to Manage or Prevent Issues:** It concerns the risk of the role of decision-maker.

But to date, the risk concept is understood as the set of possible threats (dall'Acqua, 2018), and threat assessment becomes only a part of a Risk Management Cycle.

Peter Gill (2012) describes that the terms 'threat' and 'risk' historically were distinguished as **Risk** means a 'safety' risk of accidental harm, **Threat** means a 'security' risk of intentional harm. But to date they are often conflated (see Table 1).

Table 1. Threat and risk: factors in common for which they are multiplied

PROBABILITY	HARM
Quality of knowledge: • Certainty • Quantifiable risk • Uncertainty • Ignorance	(vulnerability) • Consciousness • Appetite • Property, finance, physical security of people, etc

The only negative view of the risk derives from the fact that only a few decades ago, in the economy, only pure risks were taken into account, which is characterized by the existence of two only scenarios. In the first scenario, highly probable, there are no economic effects on the company, in the second scenario, in low probability, an event that results in a very high level of damage occurs. This notion of risk is perfectly adequate and simpler to manage the pure risks and in general of those risks characterized by a better scenario where no adverse event occurs.

The causes of adverse events are the agents of a threat, and the target or thing being threatened is the object at risk. If all possible, positive and negative scenarios are taken into account and the risk is measured by considering both positive and negative events, correct results may be obtained, otherwise, taking into account only negative aspects, it is likely to come to misguided conclusions.

Table 2. The source of threats

from the outside	from the inside
• military espionage • political-institutional espionage • economic, industrial, criminal flow	• endogenous terrorism • organized criminal groups • phenomena of separatism and indipendence requests

Today, we live new threats, for the end of traditional military threats (territory and national sovereignty), the complexity of economic and commercial relations, and because of the defense became "global" and implemented through information actions . Examples of new threats are: telematic terrorism, international terrorism, religious fanaticism, toxic waste disposal, trafficking of sex, illegal people trafficking, and as an extension, organized crime, eversion, national economic security. Examples of new wars are: bacteriological wars, cultural wars, technological wars (see Figure 1).

In the 21st century, the pinnacle of" skill "for the best of analysts is to be able to put politicians in touch with top international experts.

Correct results may be obtained:

- If all possible positive and negative scenarios are taken into account (identification)
- If the danger is measured by considering both positive and negative events

So, the support by an Intelligence activity can define and pursue a strategy to:

- identifying all the external dangers that may affect a State
- identifying possible scenarios according to interpretative approaches and, according to a SWOT analysis, can define contingent interrelations and lines of action in order to:
- maximize positive outcomes in favorable scenarios (opportunities)
- minimize negative outcomes in unfavorable scenarios (obstacles/ threats)

There are possibility of misguided conclusions. The major consequence in the risk management of this view is to neglect or underestimate the effects of extreme events. It means low probability scenarios and tremendous damage

Figure 1. Sectors of Competences of Security Intelligence in a State context of vulnerability Source:dall'Acqua, 2019)

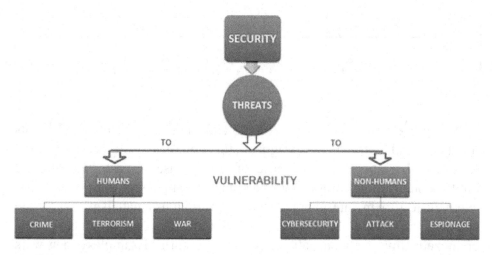

RISK IDENTIFICATION

Risk identification is the process of listing potential project risks and their characteristics. It is used for risk analysis, which in turn will support creating risk responses. Identified risks can also be represented in a **risk breakdown structure**, a hierarchical structure used to categorize potential project risks by source.

Authors propose some crucial risk identification criteria (see fig. 2).

Figure 2. Identification Criteria

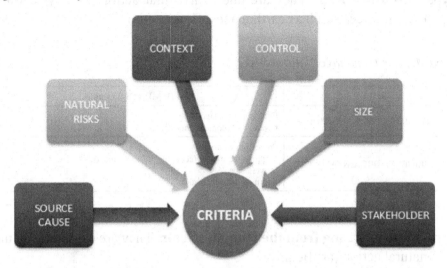

Criterion: Source or Cause

It concerns events possibly giving rise to a damage.

Type 1. **Technological Risks.** They are related to the danger for man and the environment possibly resulting from a series of productive activities, linked to infrastructure and technology networks, increasingly sophisticated and complex in equipment and installations

Table 3. How to manage Technological risks

ROLES	THEIR MEANS (examples)
POLITICAL DECISION-MAKER	Laws Rules
INTELLIGENCE ORGANIZATION	Corruption - Crimes Industrial espionage and sabotage Nuclear resources for war purposes

Type 2. **Natural Risk.** They are due to irregular actions of physical and natural forces (such as earthquakes, floods, etc.)

Table 4. How to manage Natural Risks

ROLES	THEIR MEANS (examples)
POLITICAL DECISION-MAKER	Emergency management Psycho-Sociological Impact
INTELLIGENCE ORGANIZATION	Preventive security Mapping the impact (economy, infrastructures) Sorveillance International cooperation

Type 3. **Risks arising from the Human Factor**. They are caused by an un-natural action (artificially)

Table 5. How to manage Risks by un.natural action

ROLES	THEIR MEANS (examples)
POLITICAL DECISION-MAKER	Laws Rules Penalty
INTELLIGENCE ORGANIZATION	Sorveillance

Criterion: Natural Risks

It concerns events classifiable in STATIC / DYNAMIC, REAL / SUBJECTIVE.

Type 1a. **Static Risks.** They are caused by an un-natural action (artificially): human mistakes and misunderstandings or high probability of an event (an internal weakness)

Table 6. How to manage Static risks

ROLES	THEIR MEANS (examples)
POLITICAL DECISION-MAKER	Preventive Policy (awareness)
INTELLIGENCE ORGANIZATION	Preventive security Mapping the impact (economy, infrastructures) Sorveillance International cooperation

Type 1b. **Dynamic Risks.** They are associated with changes in human needs and technological - organizational improvements

Table 7. How to manage Dynamic risks

ROLES	THEIR MEANS (examples)
POLITICAL DECISION-MAKER	Policy on the innovation Costs/Benefits analysis
INTELLIGENCE ORGANIZATION	Intelligence Cycle (high uncertainty) (see chapter 1)

Table 8. Situational awareness

STRATEGIC: PREVENTION	TACTICAL: DETECTION
Risk Management Vulnerability Management Threat Modeling	Proactive/Reactive Threat Communications Breach Discovery

Type 2a. **Objective Risks.** They are a variation related to a real loss vs a probable loss

Table 9. How to manage Objective risks

ROLES	THEIR MEANS (examples)
POLITICAL DECISION-MAKER	Policy Cycle (see chapter 1)
INTELLIGENCE ORGANIZATION	from Data to Intelligence (see chapter 1)

Type 2b. **Subjective Risks.** They are relating to the mental state of an individual who has doubts (or disturbances) about the outcome of an event, with high individual uncertainty.

Table 10. How to manage Subjective risks

ROLES	THEIR MEANS (examples)
POLITICAL DECISION-MAKER	Public advertising actions to prevent crime Professional training and support
INTELLIGENCE ORGANIZATION	Indicators to forecast (i.e. kamikaze actions) (see Table 11 and Fig. 3)

Figure 3. Clue vs Indicator

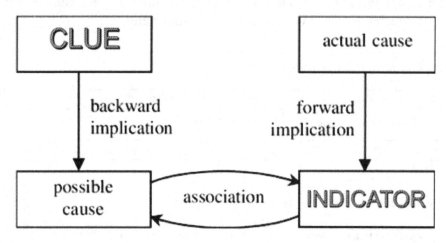

Table 11. Indicator's purpose

PURPOSE	TYPES

To establish a baseline from which to measure improvement
To monitor process performance
    Assess progress
    Determine negative trends so proactive, corrective action can be taken
To shape behavior
    To drive decisions / action
	Leading indicators
	- Predicts future performance / likely outcomes
	- Provides opportunity to take corrective action that alters the eventual outcome
	Lagging indicators
	- Reflect things that have already happened
	- "Historical record" – what happened in the past
	- No ability to alter the past outcome

Criterion: Context

It concerns the Effects of the event possibly giving rise to a damage

Type 1. **Into the human society.** They likely cause monetary losses, for example in the financial sector:
- Studies on the so-called theory of capital gains in the valuation of investments
- Studies on the perception of risk by investors
- Studies on the political dimension of risk in international affairs

Type 2. **Environmental Risks.** for example, susceptible to leakage with immediate reflection on the population, such as:
- Public risks
- Health risks: tumors, infectious diseases, etc.

- ○ Social risks: Protecting the population from social risks is the main objective of welfare policies. Social risks vary according to the social class, gender, age, but also depending on contexts

Table 12. How to manage risk into the human society / environmental risks

ROLES	THEIR MEANS (examples)
POLITICAL DECISION-MAKER	Events which are political in nature, such as revolutions, terrorist attacks, an abrupt changes in tariffs or acts of expropriation, are generally much more difficult to predict than sovereign default. Regulations can be set at all levels of government, including federal, state and local, as well as in other countries
INTELLIGENCE ORGANIZATION	Nonetheless, when it comes to political risk, in most cases a purely quantitative approach is not possible. Human judgment plays a central role. But methodologies of Intelligence Analysis, such as logit/ probit analysis, regression analysis, Monte Carlo simulations, value at risk and principal components analysis, non-parametric methods (neural networks) can be of support

Criterion: Control

It is a criterion bases on the possibility of facing and controlling the risks (more generic)

Type 1a. **Avoidable Risks.** the subject can predict and establish a control strategy

Type 1b. **Inevitable Risks.** The subject cannot avoid damage to external or internal factors

Table 13. How to manage avoidable / inevitable risks

ROLES	THEIR MEANS (examples)
POLITICAL DECISION-MAKER	It has typically been a major concern for energy and natural resources companies, which are characterized by high sunk costs and which face unavoidable. It is a case of "micro-risk". For example, diplomatic tension between two countries can be connected to events for which the citizens of the first one vandalize all the second country based companies situated in it.
INTELLIGENCE ORGANIZATION	Risk avoidance is often not an option, and the only possibility left might be trying to build up an adequate risk mitigation strategy, supported by an Intelligence Analysis (see the next paragraph about the analytical approaches)

Criterion :Size

It concerns the possibility of distinguishing threats from the size in the scope of action

Type 1a: **Large-Scale Risks,** affecting the entire society
Type 1b:: **Small-Scale Risks:** the personal activities of each individual, voluntary and controllable or not, and which have generally less catastrophic consequences than the first one

Criterion: Stakeholders

They are those who act or suffer the consequences of the unfavorable event

Type 1a: **Impersonal Risks,** in origin and effect, such as those associated with disarmament of economic systems, political-social changes, extraordinary natural disturbances
Type 1b: **Personal Risks,** in origin and effect, such as the risk of death, unemployment, property, legal liability, etc..
Type 2: **Related to individual characteristics,** such as: age, nationality gender, race, education
Type 3:. **Related to financial characteristics,** such as: wealth or income
Type 4: **Related to a job,** such as: employment,managerial activity, industrial activity or seniority

ANALYTICAL APPROACHES TO THE RISK MANAGEMENT

The main theoretical approaches to the risk management are four (Dall'Acqua, 2018), as follows.

Logic-Probabilistic Approach

The purpose of this approach is to: connect the concept of risk to situations where the result of the actions is not certain, but where the probability of alternative random results is known

It uses of probabilistic tools and can be selected according to preference relationships by the decision-maker. It is inherent in a so-called "engineering" approach, and proposes the formulation of a decision-making criterion useful in identifying and measuring uncertainty related to risky actions

Specifically, the Cost-Benefit Analysis, together with the Decision Analysis, represents an analytical risk formalization by means of the strategy-oriented formula, according to which the selection is carried out through the formal adoption of a plurality of evaluation criteria, internal and external to each single system of interaction

Cognitive Approach

The cognitive risk approach aims to counteract and define the limits of the previous notion, as it attributes the value of mere information factor to the probabilistic distribution of the event, which, together with others, contributes to determining the individual's attitude.

The risk equates to the subjective and personal perception of each individual of an objective uncertain situation: the attempt to formulate an objective method of reducing and making uncertainty over the future acceptable, in fact, conflicts with the practical impossibility of bringing in a single pattern analytic the plurality of the individual and social processes underlying it.

Systemic-Social Approach

It proposes a systemic-social concept of risk management proper to a functionalist-structuralist approach, according to which it is not an expression of the decision-making process of an individual and its behavior, but translates the dynamics of the entire social structure into an over-individual plan. Contingencies, adaptive responses to them, social order and social communication are closely related concepts.

This theoretical approach renounces the primacy of the individual, both as a rational investigator (see the logical-probabilistic notion), and as a point of reference for the scheme of action (see the cognitive-subjectivistic notion).

Socio-Cultural Approach

The socio-cultural approach stems from cognitive studies that include, among the variables of decision-making, also the decision-making opportunities offered by the environment, defining as a 'set of opportunities' the set of actions compatible with physical, economic constraints, legal, psychological, social or moral. In summary, the risk can be identified by the combination of the knowledge of possible alternatives (with respect to the future) and the sharing of objectives (or consensus). From the intersection between these two dimensions, the schema defining the constituent conditions of the risk thus arises.

CONCLUSION

A multitude of meanings attached to the term risk and there is still confusion about what political risk exactly is, and what is the best way to assess it. This holds true at every level of analysis, be the approach based on "micro" or "macro" political risk. A major challenge in this respect regards the question of how to design and conduct meta-studies of political risk assessment methodologies.

The present contribution proposes a global description of the risk management. It intends to be a theoretical as well practical guideline for policy-makers and Intelligence practitioners as decisionmakers,, to manage tasks towards goal, and to understand what elements are useful to own personal and professional development to optimize performance. The purpose is to provide cues for discussion and further research.

REFERENCES

Dall'Acqua, L. (2018). Risk Taxonomy and Strategic Rationality in Enterprise Decision-Making Process: A Metacognitive Analysis. In L. dall'Acqua & D. Lukose (Eds.), Improving Business Performance Through Effective Managerial Training Initiatives (pp. 17-45). Hershey, PA: IGI Global. doi:10.4018/978-1-5225-3906-3.ch002

Dall'Acqua, L. (2019). Scientific Intelligence, Decision-Making and Cyber-Security. In *Forecasting and Managing Risk in the Health and Safety Sectors*. IGI Global Publisher. doi:10.4018/978-1-5225-7903-8.ch002

Gill, P. (2012, April). Intelligence, Threat, Risk and the Challenge of Oversight. *Intelligence and National Security, 27*(2), 206–222. doi:10.1080/02684527 .2012.661643

KEY TERMS AND DEFINITIONS

Micro Risk: Type of political risk that refers to political actions in a host country that can adversely affect selected foreign operations. Micro risk can come about from events that may or may not be in the reigning government's control.

Political Risk: It is the risk that investment's returns could suffer as a result of political changes or instability in a country.

Risk Analysis: A proven way of identifying and evaluating factors that could negatively affect the success of an action or project. It allows you to examine the risks that you face and helps you decide whether or not to move forward with a decision.

Chapter 5

Measures of Success for Intelligence Analysis and Products

ABSTRACT

The chapter analyzed the concept of threat vs. risk, focusing on possible risks identification criteria and the main analytical approaches for risk management. It proposes an evaluation of sources as strength or weakness points, and application of cognitive biases in the intelligence analysis, and ethical issues in the intelligence activities such as politicization and secrecy issues. This research intends to put key questions and related criticalities of policy-making school, proposing a conceptual interpretation, possible strategies, and tools to manage, which can attempt to explain how intelligence analysis happens, which typically adopt company productions or cyclic modes of analysis, reducing them to a rational, objective process of steps and stages, especially to govern emergencies.

DOI: 10.4018/978-1-7998-1562-4.ch005

MAIN MEASURES OF SUCCESS FOR INTELLIGENCE PRODUCTS

Worldwide Analysts have common problems and similar challenges (threats), such as:

- understanding and interpretation of information by management of intelligence
- competition with media and other information brokers who communicate and disseminate information on world events instantaneously
- overabundance of information
- level of knowledge and application of technical analysis, scientific methodologies, tools, techniques, for different contexts, "clients" and intelligence products
- the effective use of the analysis in the decision-making process
- intelligence estimable to design future developments, allowing the development of strategic plans

Figure 1. Intelligence actions: Strength or Weakness points

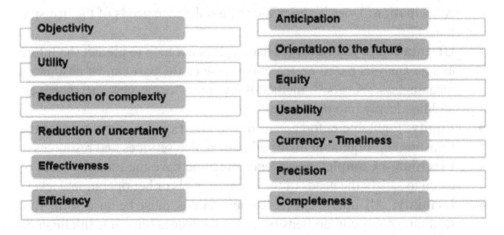

- **Reduction of Uncertainty:** It is the first meaning why Intelligence exists as a decision-support
- **Objectivity:** Often the analysis activity is influenced by preconditions related to the environment and to the organization in which the analyst

moves. Does it avoid mirror imaging, cultural bias, and prejudicial judgments? The analyst should nullify these influences. All judgments must be evaluated for the ossibility of deliberate distortions and manipulations due to Self-interest.

- **Utility:** By definition, the analyst's work should respond to the needs expressed by the ecision-making level, in a particular context. A useful methodological aid should help the analyst produce outputs related to "things necessary to know" compared to "useful things to know".

- **Reduction of Complexity:** Within the sphere of institutional intelligence, the simplest methodologies to reduce complexity to easily manageable dimensions are those of ordered classification, chronologically, or by source or by an event in order to allow an easy comprehension of the relations of cause and effect.

- **Effectiveness:** Accomplishing goals. Achieving planned and desired results

- **Efficiency:** Not wasting resources. Providing "good value for money"

- **Timeliness:** Intelligence must be delivered while the content is still actionable under the customer's circumstances

- **Currency:** It concerns the production of outcome in time for the application of the resultants.

- **Anticipation:** Does it anticipate the intelligence needs of the decision maker?

- **Orientation to the Future:** History does not help to predict the future and an analysis based on the experience of the past can be absolutely meaningless. A good methodology must open new perspectives, looking deeply into the future.

- **Equity**: Equitable enforcement of the law. Equal treatment under the Constitution. Equitable distribution of police services and resources

- **Precision – Completeness:** Does outcome have the required level of detail to satisfy the needs of the end user at his or her operational level?

- **Usability:** All intelligence communications must be in a form that facilitates ready comprehension and immediate application. Intelligence products must be compatible with the customer's capabilities for receiving, manipulating, protecting, and storing the product

EVALUATION OF SOURCES AS STRENGTH OR WEAKNESS POINTS

The assessment of all resources (such as, decisions or external events; geographical, political, cultural, economic, scientific, military, strategic or biographical issues) cannot be ignored when dealing with information.

The main needed characteristics are the relevance, accuracy and reliability.

Relevance: Information must be selected and organized for its applicability data collection must be carried out in such a way that the costs relating to this criterion are considered to be less than the benefits that may derive from it. For example, the timing that data collection needs can be not comparable with the urgent needs expressed by decision makers.

Accuracy: All sources and data must be evaluated for the possibility of technical error, misperception, and hostile efforts to mislead. The level of accuracy derives in particular from the quality of the data and information obtained during the beginning phase of the Intelligence production process.

Reliability: To better define this factor, see the description in Table 1.

Table 1. Reliability of sources

RATING	DESCRIPTION (synthesis)
Reliable	No doubt of authenticity, trustworthiness, or competency; has a history of complete reliability, usually demonstrates adherence to known professional standards and verification processes.
Usually Reliable	Minor doubt concerning authenticity, trustness, or competency; has a history of valid information most of the time; may not have a history of adherence to professionally accepted standards but generally identifies what is known
Fairly Reliable	Doubt of authenticity, trustworthiness, or competency but has provided valid information in the past.
Not Usually Reliable	Significant doubt about authenticity, trustworthiness, or competency but has provided valid information in the past.
Unreliable	Lacking in authenticity, trustworthiness, and competency; history of invalid information.
Cannot Be Judged	No basis exists for evaluating the reliability of the source; new information source.

Figure 2. Evaluation codes according to the 5x5x5 evaluation system (Source: OSCE, 2017)

	EVALUATION OF SOURCE		EVALUATION OF INFORMATION
A	Always reliable	1	Known to be true without reservation
B	Mostly reliable	2	Known personally to the source but not to the person reporting
C	Sometimes reliable	3	Not known personally to the source but corroborated
D	Unreliable	4	Cannot be judged
E	Untested source	5	Suspected to be false

COGNITIVE BIASES IN THE INTELLIGENCE ANALYSIS

As decision-makers, Intelligence analysts can fall in cognitive biases. Cognitive biases are a mistake in reasoning, evaluating, remembering, or other cognitive processes. They are mental errors caused by our simplified information processing strategies, and can be cultural, emotional or intellectual predisposition toward a certain judgment, organizational bias, and bias that results from one's own self-interest (see chapter 2). Cognitive biases are similar to optical illusions in that the error remains compelling even when one is fully aware of its nature. But an awareness of biases, by itself, does not produce a more accurate perception.

In the case of Intelligence Analysis, the main types can summarized in:

Vividness: Vivid, concrete, and personal information has a greater impact than pallid, abstract information that may actually have substantially greater value as evidence

Absence of Evidence: Estimate potential impact of missing data and adjust confidence in judgment. Using of fault trees

Oversensitivity to Consistency: "out of sight, out of mind" highly correlated or redundant information, or drawn from a very small or biased sample

Law of Small Numbers: Tendency to place too much reliance on small samples

Coping with Evidence of Uncertain Accuracy: That is Misunderstanding, misperception, incomplete story, source bias, distortion in the communication chain, misunderstanding and misperception by the analyst

Persistence of Impressions: Based on Discredited Evidence Impressions tend to persist even after the evidence that created those impressions has been fully discredited

Biases in Perception of Cause and Effect: When inferring the causes of behavior too much weight is accorded to personal qualities and dispositions of the actor and not enough to situational determinants

Bias in Favor of Causal Explanations: People expect patterned events to look patterned and random events to look random, but this is not the case. Random events often look patterned

Bias Favoring Perception of Centralized Direction: Tendency to see the actions of organizations as the intentional result of centralized direction and planning. Accidents, unintended consequences, coincidences, and small causes leading to large effects are perceived as coordinated actions, plans and conspiracies

Similarity of Cause and Effect: Rule of thumb people use is to consider the similarity between attributes of the cause and attributes of the effect. Assumption that big events have important consequences, does not apply

Internal vs. External Causes of Behavior: (Attributional bias) A fundamental error made in judging the causes of behavior is to overestimate the role of internal factors and underestimate the role of external factors

Overestimating Our Own Importance: Individuals and organizations tend to overestimate the extent to which they successfully influence the behavior of others: familiar with own efforts, much less with factors that influenced the other's decision

Illusory Correlation Correlation: Alone does not necessarily imply causation. For example, two events might co-occur because they have a common cause, rather than because one causes the other. But when two events or changes do co-occur, and the time sequence is such that one always follows the other, people often infer that the first caused the second.

ETHICAL ISSUES

Joshua Rovner, Associate Professor of Strategy and Policy at the U.S. Naval War College, identifies three types of pathology between intelligence agencies and political summit. They are negligence, excessive harmony, politicization (Rovner, 2011).

Negligence

It occurs when:

- the decision maker deliberately ignores the information and analysis coming from the Secret Services
- the decision maker selects among them only those that confirm and support their positions while ignoring those that conflict with their own ideas or political objectives

Rovner states that it occurs because the decision maker may consider them poor may have more confidence in their personal sources or analytical skills. And the decision maker tends to ignore those analyzes and information that are "psychologically disconcerting" with his own consolidated view of reality. An example was the Barbarossa Operation (the code name of the German invasion of the Soviet Union during World War II). In 1941 Stalin deliberately ignored intelligence information that alerted him to an imminent German invasion of Soviet territory considering them unreliable

Figure 3. Barbarossa Operation

Excessive Harmony

It is the opposite to the previous one. The natural and physiological tension between intelligence officials and political decision makers has completely disappeared. It occurs when:

- the intelligence does not want to contradict the decision maker
- the decision maker uncritically accepts the analyzes produced by the secret services

An example was in 1973, Syria and Egypt surprisingly attacked Israel (Yom Kippur War).

Figure 4. Yom Kippur War

Israeli political leadership having great faith in military intelligence uncritically accepted information from a high-level source within the Egyptian establishment. The risk assessment was conditioned, led to underestimate the indications of an imminent attack for an excessive harmony between policy-makers and secret services (Rovner, 2011). It is counterintuitive to think about harmony as some kind of pathology, but the effects of shared tunnel vision are disastrous. Intelligence-policy relations require a certain amount of tension to be effective. If intelligence officials are enamored of policymakers, they will be less willing to offer candid judgments that go against policy beliefs. If policymakers accept intelligence reports uncritically, their decisions may rest on shoddy logic and misperceptions.

Politicization

It means the manipulation of intelligence in order to conform it to the preferences of the decision maker. The manipulated information are used as an ex post support for a decision already made.

According to Rovner's analysis, political leaders aim to defend their positions of power to gain consensus for their political choices. To achieve these objectives, the decision maker exerts pressure (direct or indirect manipulation) on the Secret Services if he believes that the intelligence analyzes and information cause him harm.

Table 2. Types of politicization

TYPE	DESCRIPTION
Direct Manipulation	Policymakers and staff pressure intelligence agencies to produce specific findings. Alternately, they appoint malleable analysts
Indirect Manipulation	Insecure analysts provide intelligence intended to support policy decisions. This may occur if analysts suspect that their managers want to see certain findings
Embedded Assumptions	Widely held strategic assumptions and social norms constrain analysis
Intelligence Subverts Policy	Intelligence analysis publicly undermines policy decisions. Alternately, Policymakers ignore intelligence because they fear subversion
Intelligence Parochialism	Analysts tailor findings for personal or professional gain. This can cause either "intelligence to please" or subversion, depending on the analyst's goals
Bureaucratic Parochialism	Bureaucracies tailor intelligence findings to support their own interests.
Partisan Intelligence	Political parties use intelligence issues for partisan gain, usually by accusing rivals of mismanaging intelligence
Intelligence as Scapegoat	*Policymakers deride intelligence when it does not support policy decisions. In addition, intelligence is blamed for failure to predict events like surprise attacks*

FALLACY (synthesis)

R. D. Steele (2006) describes several significant negative aspects in the Intelligence action, or reasons for which the process cannot work. Following, we cite some of the mains.

Ignored Open Source Information: 80% of what we need to do intelligence is not secret, not digital, not in our language, and not owned by the government. He states that his awakening to open sources came when I spent $20 million U.S. dollars in creating the Marine Corps Intelligence Command, only to discover that 80% of what I needed to do good intelligence for my generals was not secret, not online, not in English, and not available from anyone in the U.S. Government. If 80% of what we need--including geospatial information--is openly available, then we must treat this source with respect, and devise conccepts, doctrine, budgets, and organizations competent in this core disciplinary area.

Very Limited Non-Official Cover: 80% of the "bad" boys and girls recruited/monitored for clandestine operations do not attend "Embassy cocktail parties". It is a huge honor to be a clandestine case officer. These are t he Jesuit priests of the holy world of intelligence. They take great risks and rarely receive proper recognition. However, to ask clandestine case officers to do what they do using only official cover, working out of official installations that are easily monitored by both hostile governments as well as hostile non-state actor groups including terrorists, is irresponsible. In America we have been lazy and cheap about this. We have also failed to properly explore multilateral clandestine operations in which our allies provide better clandestine case officers than we can grow.

Almost no Technical Processing: If we do not process what we have collected (generally at great expense) we might as well not collect it at all. We will talk about Processing in the next three slides,so for now I will simply observe that it is foolish to spend money or take risks to collect information that is not processed. We can double or triple the value of collection if we add open sources in 31+ languages to our inputs, and we can double or triple the value of what we collect if we process it using modern technology to digitize, visualize, and store what we know. Sense-making matters. We do not do it—Able Danger was a good start, but destroyed for the wrong reasons.

No Data Standards: Data standards (for instance, XML) are vital if we are to be able to exploit modern information technology.

No Geospatial Attributes: Automated "all-source fusion" is not possible unless every datum, in every medium, has both a time and a geospatial attribute

No Interoperability or All-Source Mixing: There must be one single processing agency where everything can be mixed and evaluated.

Emphasis on Security Instead of Answers: Intelligence is about decision-supporting. Must not confuse expertise, foreign languages, and security clearances nor should we require that the same person have them all

Failure to Impact on Policymaker Awareness: Policymakers are loosely-educated and often dismiss the value of global knowledge. Intelligence is most valuable to the public interest when it constantly educates policymakers in a compelling manner

Failure to Win Public Support for Intelligence: Intelligence is not taught in schools and there is no public appreciation for its vital contributions. We must establish a public discipline of intelligence across the seven tribes and in the public eye.

AGENTS OF INFLUENCE

Usually, agents of influence are distinguished into three main categories: a controlled agent, a trusted contact and an unwitting agent. The first one is recruited and is subordinate to the agency, the second one wittingly collaborates with the foreign power on the voluntary basis but is not officially aligned with the agency and the third one does not have any idea that his/her actions contribute to the interests of the foreign power, so-called "useful idiot". (Shultz – Godson, 1984).

The prototype of the modern-day agents of influence can be found in Soviet Russia's so-called fellow-travelers. Those were people who during the period from the Bolshevik Revolution in 1917 onwards sympathized to a greater or lesser extent with the policies of the Soviet Union but never joined the Communist party. Fellow-travelers involved a broad range of committed individuals with common political views, they were mainly art workers or people of creative professions, for example, French author André Gide, German theatre practitioner Bertolt Brecht, Chilean poet and politician Pablo Neruda and so on. (Rosenberg, 1973).

The essence of the fellow-travelers concept is a perfect analogy for agents of influence today who are known not to have any formal relations with the foreign power, that is why they are hard and almost impossible to detect by the counter-intelligence for the lack of concrete proof. (Girling, 1984.

Intuitively, activities of the agent of influence are so abstract and intangible that it becomes unreasonable to accuse people of their views even if they are controversial.

The age of technology and electronic communication contributes even more to the spread of information and fake news than it was a century or decades ago. The radicalization of masses can be now realized easier due to the high number of different media, also conspiracy media and the ones with a low level of credence. This is the moment when an agent of influence enters the process to propose his/her arguments and factual evidence to support or oppose the abovementioned event.

As an example, the "agent of influence" concept has seen its rise during the bipolar confrontation of the Cold War period. Agents of influence belonged either to the American CIA or Soviet KGB, although the USSR was better known for the more active applying of the idea to real life. Historical Dictionary of International Intelligence also points out that the term is mainly used "to describe covert supporters of the Soviet Union during the Cold War, they were often in positions of trust and not instantly recognized, through overt party membership or as actively engaged in promoting the communist cause."(West, 2015) So the term itself came to be coined with Soviet attempts to discredit hostile governments and it is important to note that this type of intelligence activity remains an essential tool in modern-day Russia as well. Already in 1974 American journalist and investigative writer John Barron claimed that "the most insidious and sometimes most dangerous KGB intrigue involves the exploitation of what the Russians call agents of influence. Through them the Soviet Union endeavors to develop its disguised voices in foreign governmental, political, journalistic, business, labor, artistic and academic circles. While agents of influence may incidentally transmit intelligence, their overriding mission is to alter opinion and policy in the interests of the Soviet Union. No activity of the KGB abroad has higher priority than its efforts to manipulate the thought and action of other nations by insinuating such agents into positions of power."(Barron, 1974, p.26) This corresponded with the general ideology of the Soviet Union during the 20th century when the idea of the expansion of the socialist revolution worldwide was a dominant feature in Soviet foreign policy. Soviet interference in the internal affairs of other states has been the issue of the active debate for a long time. It is being claimed that Soviet (Pryce-Jones, 1995).

REFERENCES

Girling, O. (1984, Summer). Article. *Vanguard, 13*(5/6), 41–42.

Marrin, S. (2011). The 9/11 Terrorist Attacks: A Failure of Policy Not Strategic Intelligence Analysis. *Intelligence and National Security, 26*(2-3), 2–3, 182–202. doi:10.1080/02684527.2011.559140

Marrin, S. (2017). *Why strategic intelligence analysis has limited influence on American foreign policy.* Routledge. doi:10.1080/02684527.2016.1275139

OSCE Organization for Security and Co-operation in Europe. (2017). *Guidebook* (Vol. 13). Intelligence-Led Policing.

Pryce-Jones, D. (1995). *The Strange Death of the Soviet Empire.* Henry Holt & Co.

Rosenberg, B., & McKibben, W. (1973). The Prediction of Systematic and Specific Risk in Common Stocks. *Journal of Financial and Quantitative Analysis, 8*(2), 317–333. doi:10.2307/2330027

Rovner, J. (2009). *Intelligence-Policy Relations and the Problem of Politicization.* Academic Press.

Rovner, J. (2011). *Fixing the Facts: National Security and the Politics of Intelligence.* Ithaca, NY: Cornell University Press.

Steele, R. (2006). *The Failure of 20th Century Intelligence.* HOPE 6.

KEY TERMS AND DEFINITIONS

Decision-Making: The result of cognitive and emotional processes, which determine the selection of a course of action among different alternatives.

Intelligence Politicization: It occurs when intelligence analysis is skewed, either deliberately or inadvertently, to give policymakers the results they desire.

Section 2
Technologies of Support

Chapter 6
Intelligence Analysis Sources:
From HUMINT to TECHINT

ABSTRACT

Intelligence is a tool, a goal, a means of assessing the weaknesses of a state in order to protect its security. Intelligence organizations support the policy process because policymakers and decision-makers constantly need tailored and timely intelligence that will provide background, context, information, and warning, as well as an assessment of the risks, benefits, and the likely outcomes. They avoid strategic unexpected threats, forces, events, and developments that are capable of threatening a nation's existence and provide long-term expertise and stability to political appointees and decision-makers. They maintain the secrecy of information, needs, and methods from disclosure to competitors or counterparts. Government agencies are allowed by law to obtain information through interception and other technical measures. This chapter focuses on the intelligence collection, the different sectors of applications, and methods.

INTRODUCTION

In every age, diplomats, spies and betrayers have been crucial pawns in the decisions on war and peace. The oldest Intelligence Organization was in Military sector. Mainly, it was thought:

DOI: 10.4018/978-1-7998-1562-4.ch006

- to understand the intentions of enemies and antagonists as a prevention aimed at defense
- to identify the opposing armed force (such as military installations, manufacturing industries, depots) for the prevention of a possible attack
- to know the territory for army moving

A "source" is any source of information: the human informant, the company database, satellite photography, telephone interception and so on, are the same generic term. In a wide range of sources, they are categorized in terms of various "INTs".

Figure 1. "INTs"

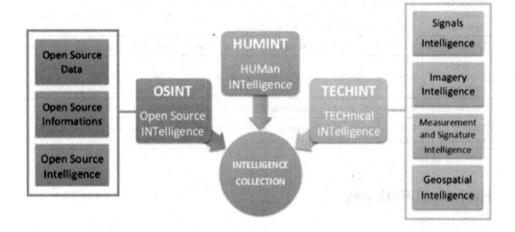

HUMINT

HUMINT can refer to a clandestine acquisition of different materials by diplomatic people, debriefing of foreign nationals and citizens who travel abroad official contacts with foreign governments. Historically it was the only source of all the Intelligence collected, that was above all the informant or the infiltrator in the enemy camp, when this was the only way to obtain information from the opposing camp. All espionage, first among the allies and the Nazi block, then between the two blocks of the Cold War, was based on the figure of the informant, the defector, the infiltrator.

It uses human sources as a tool with a variety of collection methods both passively and actively to gather information, to satisfy the commander's intelligence requirements and cross-cue other intelligence disciplines, to identify elements, intentions, composition, strength, dispositions, tactics, equipment, personnel, and capabilities.

Table 1. Main HUMINT functions

TYPE	DESCRIPTION
Debriefings	It's the systematic questioning of individuals by direct and indirect questioning techniques.
Screening	It's the process of evaluating and selecting human and media sources, based on the probability of a particular source having priority information and the degree of difficulty of extracting that information from the source.
HUMINT Contact Operations.	It's tactically oriented, that closely use human sources (on the stage) to identify attitude, intentions, composition, strength, dispositions, tactics, equipment, target development, personnel, and capabilities to forecast an imminent danger.
Liaison	It's to obtain information of interest and to coordinate or deconflict HUMINT activities
Document Exploitation (DOCEX)	It's the systematic extraction of information from all media formats
Interrogation	It's the systematic effort to procure information by direct and indirect questioning techniques
Tactical questioning	It's the expedient initial questioning for information of immediate tactical value to provide critical information for situational understanding

Historical Pathway

The first "Information Service" was based on specially designated personnel, able to assess what the important information was by inclination or specific training (Lowenthal, 2003).

Herodotus (484 – 430 B.C.) narrated how the Second Persian War had failed due to a Greek informant introduced into the Persian court.

He had learned of the invasion plan sent a slave home with a bar of virgin wax whose wooden support was painted the warning message for Sparta.

Figure 2. A bar of wax

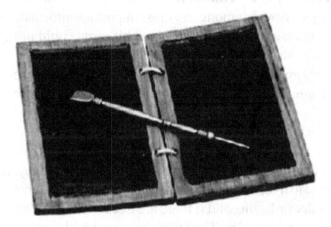

Caesar, in the De Bello Gallico (58/50 B.C.), declares how the documents useful for the Gallia campaign were encrypted using the transliteration method where each letter was replaced by another. It's the first example of cryptography. The word cryptography comes from the union of two Greek words: κρυπτός (kryptós) which means "hidden", and γραφία (graphía) which means "writing". Cryptography is about methods to make a message "obfuscated" so that it is not intelligible to unauthorized people to read it. Such a message is commonly called cryptogram.

Figure 3. Hannibal

In the III century B.C., **Hannibal,** against Rome, infiltrated his agents in Northern Italy obviously among the most important information that had to report: the mountain passes through which his army could proceed with the cavalry and with the elephants.

A first problem arose: the need of lots money to pay information.

Gengis Khan, in the 13th century, employed explorers for reconnaissance used "agents" appropriately infiltrated to spread rumors about his cruelty and his audacity.

As well as, into the Old Testament, it is written: "They observe the nature of the land if the people who live there are strong, few or many, if it's an easy or difficult land to live, if the cities are weakly defended or if they are fortified, if the earth is dry or fertile, and if there are trees or not ". "Meraghelim" was the name of informers, spies. They were equipped with torches and relays as tools of communication and used special reconnaissance units to scour the land and capture prisoners to interrogate (Singh 2001).

Sun Tzu, in the IV BC, wrote in the "Art of War": *"What enables the sensible sovereign and the good general to strike and conquer and achieve the goals is the precognition which was the foundation of the ability to make predictions"*:

- Spies must have great intuition and a keen mind
- You must be straight forward with your spies and treat them kindly
- You must be wise in order to interpret the truth from false reports
- Be clever with espionage missions and use them in all warfare
- If secret information is uncovered by the spy before the time is ripe, he must be put to death along with the man to whom the secret was told

"The enemy's spies who have come to spy on us must be sought out, tempted with bribes, led away and comfortably housed. Thus they will become double agents and available for our service. It is through the information brought by the double agent that we are able to acquire and employ local and inward spies. It is owing to his information, again, that we can cause the doomed spy to carry false tidings to the enemy" (Art of War)[1].

Mithridates, VIII king of Pontus from 111 BC, organized the biggest Information activity in the ancient age, creating a real "staff intelligence made up of one man". He was an intellectual genius, speaking 22 languages. He was concerned with gathering the necessary information in first person, crossing Asia Minor on foot. During the first century BC his army constituted the most serious threat to Roman hegemony in the Mediterranean. However, the knowledge that Mithridates had of the enemy was superior to the one he had of the internal threat: he didn't foresee a mutiny among the ranks of his army.

During the Roman Era, **General Suetonius Paulinus,** Roman Official in the 62 AD, with only 10,000 men defeat 230,000 Britons also thanks to the collection of significant information, made on the ground and on the inhabitants.

Figure 4. General Suetonius Paulinus
(Source: http://www.tscm.com/suntzu.html)

Edward III of England, before the battle of Crecy (1346), during the 100 years war, he had very little strategic information available. This was the way wars were conducted.Military campaigns were usually based on a series of fights in which the leaders' personalities, their tactical audacity, their systems of infantry, cavalry and artillery use were known to the contenders.

Gustavo Adolfo of Sweden, king of Sweden from 1611 to 1632, was an innovator in the field of information. He added a "Chief of the Explorers", anticipating the analogous "Intelligence staffs" of the French and German armies for about a century.

In the mid-sixteenth century, one of the first cases of strategic information activity conducted by a private agency was the activity carried out by the various **Banks** in Europe. "Strategic Intelligence" carried out by western traders AND merchants, to get:

- economic data
- habits and customs
- political information
- communication routes of peoples and European
- countries

decisive for the success or failure of their companies.

Since the seventeenth century, there are few news on the systematic production of strategic information from part of **government services**.

Instead we have news that testify the use and production of strategic information by **private institutions**.

Friederich The Great, third king of Prussia and the elector prince of Brandenburg from 1740 to 1786, usually said that the knowledge of a country is, for a General, what a rifle is for a jack, and the rules of arithmetic are for a quantity surveyor.

George Washington, an American political leader, military general, statesman, and Founding Father, was know for:

- recruiting spies and a number of agents
- setting up spy rings
- devising secret methods of reporting
- analyzing raw intelligence
- mounting an extensive campaign to deceive the British

" *The necessity of procuring good intelligence is apparent and need not be further urged.... For upon Secrecy, success depends in most Enterprises of the kind, for want of it, they are generally defeated, however well planned.. .. " (Washington G., letter to Colonel Elias Dayton, 26 July 1777)*

In November 1775-1776, the Continental Congress created the Committee of Secret Correspondence. This committee gathered foreign intelligence from people in Ireland, England, and elsewhere in Europe to help prosecute the war. President Washington requested Congress to provide funds to finance intelligence operations.

In July 1790, the Congress established the Contingent Fund of Foreign Intercourse (also known as the Secret Service Fund). $40,000 was authorized for this purpose. Within three years the fund had grown to $1 million, or 12 percent of the Government's budget.

During the War of 1812, the Secretary of War refused to believe the British would invade Washington. Military Intelligence (MI) reported from this perspective. It was a significant failure in MI.

Until the second half of the XIX century, the scenes of **European espionage** were dominated by individuals willing to work simultaneously for several clients.

As an example, the Italy's - war of 1866, the first fought after the proclamation of the Kingdom of Italy, was characterized by a general ignorance about the enemy to face, his intentions and movements, his strengths and abilities.

At the same time, France, in 1886, was the first country that regulates espionage offenses with a specific law, but the penalties are relatively mild. The mobilization plans considered as a base that:

- the fundamental information is the troop concentration technique, to evaluate the opponent's numerical weight
- the plan to transfer the armies to their place of using low penalty: for foreign agents discovered in action on the territory of the Habsburg monarchy, the maximum sentence consisted of five years of imprisonment the territory in which he will have to operate

During **the Great War,** a preventive defense of internal security, and a defense of security from the outside were organized. These actions had as goals: disinformation, sabotage, a political, economic and cultural interference.

The Great War provides the opportunity for the Intelligences of the various powers to refine the great and still crude game of espionage:

- the British plot in the Middle East
- the Russians infiltrate Constantinople
- the Italians violate the secrets of Vienna
- Austrian saboteurs blow up the battleships Benedetto Brin and Leonardo da Vinci

Anne Marie Lesser, aka **Fraulein Doktor**, alias 1-4GW, is the woman who with Mata Hari divides the limelight of espionage able to subtract from the "Deuxième Bureau" the list of French agents in neutral countries.

Figure 5. Anne Marie Lesser

At the end of the conflict, the British Security Intelligence Service (SIS) the American Office of Strategic Service (OSS), working closely together, succeeded in recruiting some German agents who, in their double-play activity, managed to deceive the their organization Intelligence ("*Abwehr*"), communicating an imminent invasion of the Balkans ally of Italy. Following this information the Germans strengthened the Balkan defenses by weakening those in Sicily.

From the end of **the Second World War**, strategic information is not just military information. Counter-information is not just a police task. Organizational models are not military or police.

Starting from the **dissolution of the Soviet empire** enormous development of IT (information technology), the Intelligence services have started to move more and more towards a search for information obtained through sophisticated electronic equipment and through the exploitation of the interconnection network global (i.e. Internet).

In the XI century, Intelligence is a fundamental mean for understanding the evolution of world society. The concept of national security has changed. We are facing a "war without limits" in which States must appeal to every citizen to ensure national security and well-being, every citizen must be a collector, producer and user of "intelligence" (Steele, 2000).

L. Longo (2003) defined a method, called I.B.A., through which all the information necessary to frame the operator is formalized. In particular, the physical and aesthetic characteristics, the state of health, the personal and family history, character and temperament, ideological assumptions, social behavior and habits, work and the social environment are analyzed. For each of these characteristics, a detailed list of the information to be acquired is presented, giving a complete picture of the "spy" profile.

TECHINT

The gathering of information through technological tools began during the First World War with the first aerial photographs of the enemy camp and continued its run up to the present day, becoming the first source of supply. The progress of technology then opened up other avenues for information gathering simultaneous transfer of communication.Nowadays, any human communication is virtually interceptable and can be acquired by anyone. The problem is how to deal with the huge amount of data collected how to identify important information.

Table 3. Main types of Technical Intelligence

TYPE	DESCRIPTION
Signals Intelligence (SIGINT)	the Intelligence of the interception of the signal (and therefore of the communications). It comprises: • communications intelligence (COMINT) • electronic intelligence (ELINT) • foreign instrumentation signals intelligence (FISINT) The main problem is an enormous amount of signal and information, that needs a further strong investment on the technologies of classification and cataloging of the information. The human resources required to translate and understand the ultimate meaning of what is intercepted
Imagery Intelligence (IMINT)	it includes representations of objects reproduced electronically or by optical means on film, electronic display devices, or other media. Imagery can be derived from visual photography, radar sensors, infrared sensors, lasers, and electro-optics.
Measurement and Signature Intelligence (MASINT)	it is intelligence data technically derived from different images than SIGINT. It employs a broad group of disciplines including nuclear, optical, radio frequency, acoustics, seismic, and materials sciences. Information derived from measurements of physical phenomena intrinsic to an object or event MASINT collectors include, but are not limited to: • *Electro-Optical*: examples infrared, laser, spectral Radar Polarimetric, High-Power or Unintentional Radio Frequency Emanations • *Geo-Physical*: examples seismic, acoustic, magnetic, gravimetric, infrasonic • *Chemical, Biological, Nuclear Biometrics*: relies on unique signatures of human beings
Geospatial Intelligence (GEOINT)	It is the ability to describe, understand, and interpret to anticipate the human impact of an event or action within a spatiotemporal environment. it is the analysis and visual representation of security-related activities on Earth. It is produced through an integration of imagery, imagery intelligence, and geospatial information. Geospatial Intelligence or "GEOINT" is actionable knowledge, a process, and a profession. It is the ability to identify, collect, store, and manipulate data, to create geospatial knowledge through critical thinking, geospatial reasoning, analytical techniques.

OSINT

OSINT concerns available information that are open to public access. The analyst at this stage of data collection takes on a dual role:

- has the task of determining the type of data necessary, the way of collecting, the data itself
- once the information has been collected, the actual analysis work begins i.e. the transformation of the information into Intelligence, or information validated, interpreted and ready to be passed to the political level

Figure 6. Information

overtly (openly)

covertly (secretly)

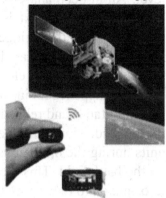

The NATO OSINT Handbook (Kernan, 2001) identifies four different categories of open information and intelligence:

- **Open Source Data** are a complex area of primary reference sources, such as photographs, images, documents, audio and video recordings, satellite images, oral debriefing, etc.
- **Open Source Information** are a secondary raw data emerged and appropriately filtered by the analysis of OSD data. They are generally composed of raw data that can be agglomerated with an editing process.
- **Open Source Intelligence** is an information derived from a voluntary process of analysis, filtering, distillation and dissemination to a specific selected category, suitable to meet particular information needs
- **Validated OSINT** (OSINT-V) is the "enhanced version" of the previous one. It basically means that a person or a team with access to other typology of classified information finds a confirmation, indeed a validation from open source information.

The main problems are always related to the overabundance of data, which often makes it difficult, if not impossible, to retrieve the desired information.

The power of OSINT at the strategic level can neither be exaggerated nor underestimated for the simple reason that it harnesses the distributed intelligence of the whole earth, in real time as well in historical memory time, across all languages and cultures. There is not a bureaucracy in the world that can match its networked power (Steele, 2007, p. 114).

For what concerns the operational level, according to what Steele argued, OSINT is still a relevant tool because it can be used to understand the theatre level. An in-deep analysis of the social, religious or security issues of the operation zone context is paramount to pave the way to a well-planned operation. And this bridges the gap between the strategic and the tactical level, the mission area applications are plenty such as Civil affairs, PSYOPs, target, terrain analysis etc. (Steele, 2004).

What happened for instance during the invasion of Iraq shows clearly both the importance and related risks of open sources at the tactical level. When the embedded journalist Geraldo Rivera, who was following some American units during the operations, disclosed their position and future movements on the battlefield. This fact could have potentially given important tactical information to the enemy from a common open source.

Social Media Intelligence (SOCMINT)

Measuring and understanding the visage of millions of people digitally arguing, talking, joking, condemning and applauding is of wide and tremendous value to many fields, interests and industries. A family of 'big data' approaches already exists to make sense of social media.

Omand et al. (2014) argue that intelligence agencies have the responsibility to follow this new event even creating a new Int named SOCMINT. They specifically stated that *"The fundamental purpose of intelligence – including SOCMINT – has been defined as being to improve the quality of decision-making by reducing ignorance"* (p.25).

They believe that SOCMINT will be able to give a realistic situational awareness to a decision maker, give a satisfying explanation of the events both for national security and law enforcement agencies and institutions. Eventually, they will be used even to plan and answer to the common questions *what if, what next and where next.* But to be effective they said that some expedient should be made, especially those useful to adapt to the nature of social media such as the deep knowledge of the different communities online and the characteristics of the different users.

Ostrovsky (2015) shows a tactical problem for the Russian Federation army after the intervention in eastern Ukraine which only in these days it has been able to fix. It was by banning the use of smartphones to its service members who will be allowed to use, since now, only "dumb phones" (Toler, 2019). Ostrovsky followed the little online crumbs of a simple rank and files Russian service member with Asian ethnicity (this detail was useful to distinguish him and his comrades from the local rebels). and followed them across Russia, eastern Ukraine and the hometown of the soldier in a Russian oblast at the borders with Mongolia. The journalist did exactly the same itinerary made by the soldier taking a selfie in the same way the soldier did. He identified the location of the home base of his unit, its location after the redeployment near the border with Ukraine and eventually some photos made on the battlefield. The presence of the units was confirmed by the locals who identified it by saying that it was different from the local rebels because they were wearing uniforms with a white armband without unit insignias and last but not least they were all of the Asian ethnicity.

Looking at the current SOCMINT technologies now on the horizon the following capabilities could for example contribute in the future to public security (Omand et al, 2012).

- **Crowd-sourced Information:** With access to social media, citizens can become active journalists, providing and relaying information from the ground. A messaging service on West Midlands Police's website allows citizens to post messages and questions in real-time, as well as allows people to identify pictures of suspects uploaded to the site. The open-source platform Ushahidi has allowed large groups of people to provide collective testimony on everything from the earthquake in Haiti to blocked roads in Washington, DC.
- **Research and Understanding:** Research based on social media could contribute to our understanding of a number of phenomena. Beneath the tactical and operational level, a background of more generic and distanced understanding is important for security work. For instance, the British counter-terrorism strategy aims to reduce the threat from terrorism so that people can go about their normal lives, freely and with confidence, and it is understood that the long-term way to do this is through tackling the underlying social, ideational and political causes of terrorism. As well as the application of geo-location techniques, for example, support a constantly evolving map showing spikes in possible violence-related tweets, facilitating a faster, more effective, and more agile emergency response.
- **Insight Into Groups:** The police could use SOCMINT to spot new, rapidly emerging 'hot topics' that spring up within group-specific conversations and how the group reacts to a specific, perhaps volatile, event. Through these and other techniques, SOCMINT might indicate

the overall levels of anger within a group, and their key concerns and themes that animate intra-group discussions. At a higher level of specificity, information can also be identified and extracted regarding when a group is planning demonstrations or flash mobs, which could lead to violence or increasing community tensions, which could change the kind of policing required to maintain public order.

- **Identification of Criminal Intent or Criminal Elements:** The law enforcement could use the warranted surveillance of social media use by individuals suspected of involvement in a crime or criminal conspiracy, the cross referencing of such individuals' accounts, the identification of accomplices, the uncovering of assumed identities, the identification of criminal networks that operate through social media sites, and the provision of social media content suspected of being evidence of a crime to the Crown Prosecution Service.

CONCLUSION

The best intelligence activity comes from using the latest technology. This chapter provides an overview of the Intelligence collection, which refers to the means and processes used to gather and 'collect' information of value, such as TECHINT (TECHnical INTelligence), OSINT (Open Source INTelligence), SOCINT (SOCial INTelligence), and HUMINT (HUMan INTelligence).

REFERENCES

Kernan, W. F. (2001). *NATO Open source Intelligence Handbook*. Retrieved from http://www.au.af.mil/au/awc/awcgate/nato/osint_hdbk.pdf

Longo, L. M. (2003). Il fattore umano nel controspionaggio industriale. In Dispense Master in Intelligence and Security (2nd ed.). Univesity of Malta.

Lowenthal, M. M. (2003). *From Secrets to Policy*. CQ Press.

Omand, D., Bartlett, J., & Miller, C. (2012). Introducing social media intelligence (SOCMINT). *Intelligence and National Security*, *27*(6), 801–823. doi:10.1080/02684527.2012.716965

Ostrovsky, A. (2015). *The Invention of Russia: The Journey from Gorbachev's Freedom to Putin's War*. Paperbacks. Atlantic Books.

Singh, S. (2011). *The Code Book: The Secrets Behind Codebreaking*. Paperback.

Steele R.D. (2000). *On Intelligence: Spies and Secrecy in an Open World*. AFCEA.

Steele, R. D. (2004). Information Peacekeeping ad the Future of Intelligence. *International Journal of Intelligence and CounterIntelligence*, *17*(2), 2. doi:10.1080/08850600490274917

Steele, R. D. (2007). Foreign Liaison and Intelligence Reform: Still in Denial. *International Journal of Intelligence and CounterIntelligence*, *20*(1), 1. doi:10.1080/08850600600889480

Toler, A. (2019). *Russia's "Anti-Selfie Soldier Law": Greatest Hits and Implications*. Retrieved from: https://www.bellingcat.com/news/uk-and-europe/2019/02/20/russias-anti-selfie-soldier-law-greatest-hits-and-implications/

ADDITIONAL READING

dall'Acqua, L. (2019). Scientific Intelligence, Decision-Making and Cyber-Security. In *Forecasting and Managing Risk in the Health and Safety Sectors*. IGI Global.

KEY TERMS AND DEFINITIONS

HUMINT: Human intelligence is derived from human sources. Usually, HUMINT remains synonymous with espionage and clandestine activities, but, in reality, most HUMINT collection is performed by overt collectors such as diplomats and military attaches.

Intelligence Analysis: Intelligence is the product resulting from the collection, collation, evaluation, analysis, integration, and interpretation of collected information.

Intelligence Collection: It is the second step of the intelligence cycle. It includes both acquiring information and provisioning that information to processing and production elements. In most cases, the development of an intelligence product involves collecting information from a number of different sources. In some cases, information may be disseminated immediately upon collection based upon operational necessity and potential impact on current operations.

Intelligence Cycle: It is the process through which intelligence is obtained, produced, and made available to users.

OSINT: Open source intelligence involves the use of materials available to the public by intelligence agencies and other adversaries.

TECHINT: It is the intelligence activity derived from the collection, processing, analysis, and exploitation of data and information pertaining to foreign equipment and materiel for the purposes of preventing technological surprise, assessing foreign scientific and technical capabilities, and developing countermeasures designed to neutralize an adversary's technological advantages.

Chapter 7
Cyber Intelligence and Security:
State of the Art

ABSTRACT

Knowledge society is characterized by a hyper-dynamic knowledge, continuously subject to review and discussion, shared, cross-media-based, with multiple reference points and an overload of information. What types of information are at risk? So many, such as power delivery, communications, aviation, financial services, medical records, criminal records, business plans. The threat posed to nations from terrorists is no longer just physical but also expands to our digital world. The benefits of the information age are numerous, but nascent threats like transnational cyber terrorism and information warfare exist alongside the positive aspects of globalization. A new challenge has emerged for free societies: democracies must find ways to strike a balance between allowing internet freedom on one hand and maintaining adequate early warning and monitoring systems on the other. These systems, combined with expanded cybersecurity cooperation across borders, will be integral in detecting suspicious digital activities and countering attempted acts of cyber warfare and cyber terrorism.

DOI: 10.4018/978-1-7998-1562-4.ch007

INTRODUCTION

During the information age, the Internet has facilitated dramatic increases in worldwide interconnectivity and communication. This form of globalization has yielded benefits, such as improved standards of living in the developing world, but it has also given rise to new weapons of resistance for groups seeking to oppose certain political measures and ideologies. The cyberspace is a new domain of operations, vital to national security. States are into an increasingly interconnected world with a diverse threat spectrum with little understanding of how decisions are made within this amorphous domain.

Cyberspace is a type of communication, indipendent from physical distance. It's an imaginary area without limits where you can meet people and discover information about any subject. It's an electronic medium used to form a global computer network and to facilitate online communication.

William Gibson in the novel Neuromancer (1984) defines it as "a consensual hallucination, experienced daily by billions of legitimate operators, in every nation, by children being taught mathematical concepts...A graphical representation of data abstracted from the banks of every computer in the human system. Unthinkable complexity. Lines of light ranged in the non-space of the mind, clusters and constellations of data" (Gibson,1989).

Cyber security is the activity of protecting information and information systems (networks, computers, data bases, data centres and applications) with appropriate procedural and technological security measures (Tonge et al, 2013).

Cyber threat intelligence (CTI) is an area of cyber security that focuses on the collection and analysis of information about current and potential attacks that threaten the safety of an organization or its assets. The first case of cyber espionage occurred more than a half-century ago, with the arrest of an East German spy in IBM's German by West Germany's police in 1968.

Since then, many cases arose and the issue of cyber security becomes more and more important and relevant. With the rise of new technologies - social networks, extended reality, internet of things - new potential threats are available, and therefore the need to protect information with new methods and tools is increasing.

Figure 1. Cyber space
(Source: https://www.geopolitica.info/the-cyberspace-il-dominio-dalla-difficile-regolamentazione/)

Risk management assumes crucial importance in cybersecurity. The cybersecurity challenges for an analyst can be summarized as:

- concepts such as convenience, functionality, usability vs security
- the Internet has become the primary virtual environment for communicating
- the exponential growth of data traffic (Big data)
- new technologies give rise to new opportunities.

Cyberterrorism

By definition, cyber terrorism means to damage information, computer systems, data, that result in harm against non-combatant targets.

The boundaries between acts of cyber terrorism, cyber crime, 'Hacktivism' are often interlinked.

Hacker profiling deals with the analysis and establishment of the personal, socio-demographic, character and psychological profiles of the organizers of a cyber attack.On the basis of the psychological aspects and the motivations that drive them to act, it is possible to distinguish hackers in 5 categories:

1. **Casual Attackers**: They tend to be motivated by curiosity and gratified by the simple possibility of using the subscriptions of others on paid sites;

2. **Political Attackers**: They militate in favor of a cause and their attacks, as well as their knowledge and experience, arise from adherence to an ideal. In this category there is a rational as well as an emotional dimension; they act mainly in order to make their ideal public;

3. **Organized Crime**: It is made up of attackers in general, professionals and sector experts who therefore hardly leave traces of their work and whose motivations are substantially of an economic nature having as their goal the profit;

4. **Squatters**: They are characterized by the impersonality of their attacks because their objectives are often independent of the recipient and the identity of the owner of the attacked system, the reasons that lead to the cyber attack, in fact, tend to became, not necessarily for criminal purposes;

5. **Insiders and Intruders**: The attacks attributable to this type can be carried out either from the inside, that is from the operators or internal users to an organization or to a computer system (insiders), both from the outside, or from external attackers, which are illegally introduced into an organization (intruders).

Depending on objectives and execution methods it is possible to identify three types of hackers:

- **Crackers:** Those whose sole objective is the destruction or serious damage to computer systems or sites through the introduction of viruses. They have high level of technical skills and mean higher level attackers, with a large knowledge and experience

- **Hackers:** Those who show their skill in entering hard-to-penetrate systems. They are medium level attackers. **Rodents** are hackers with a very low level of technical skills, able to create little damage or chaos

- **Hackers of Different Connotations**: They are subjects who use technology for purposes other than gambling, such as *lucrative hackers* (the intrusion is carried out by competitors of a company to modify or recover commercially valuable files), the *tecnovandals* (the attack is motivated only by destructive desire, the mode used is the Denial of Service to render the services used by the predestined victim useless), the *cyber-terrorists* (the attack is directed to circuits of political interest for revolutionary or religious reasons) and the *lammers* (those that do not create, but use programs made by real hackers).

In general, for **computer forensics** we could indicate that technical-investigative activity aimed at identifying, acquiring, preserving, managing, analyzing and interpreting of digital traces, which can be found in computers or electronic devices, as well as their correlation with facts, circumstances, hypotheses and traces of any nature, found or in any case relating to the investigated fact (Tonellotto,, 2014).

The purpose of computer forensics is also to interpret the data present on the computer, without however limiting itself to a simple systematic analysis of an engineering type, but also and above all taking into account the context investigated, the acquired clues, the elements and hypotheses formulated in the course of the investigations. Therefore, by correlating the various elements it is possible to contextualize the computer data, making it a source of evidence that can be used in an investigative and procedural context in order to obtain an optimal probative picture.

The traces detected on a computer do not always allow to establish an accusation about the commission of a computer crime due to the possibility of remaining in the typical Internet anonymity; however, at the same time, the Internet presents as a second side of the coin the almost total impossibility of totally erasing the traces of its own conduct.

Many indispensable national activities such as transport, telephony, media, air defense, banking, scientific research, institutional and government activities can only be explained by digital technology and computer networks.

It is therefore obvious that their sabotage by a terrorist could put an entire nation in a state of total blackout within a few hours. Therefore, if society has reached very high levels of organization from one side, it presents a greater number of weak links in the computer chain than in the past, thus becoming an easy target for a new kind of terrorism, set in place with no more weapons. fire but with computer keyboards.

Sophisticated and virtually untraceable political "hacktivists" possess the ability to disrupt or destroy government operations, banking transactions, city power grids, and even military weapon systems. Fortunately, western countries banded together to effectively combat the Estonian cyber attacks and minimize their effects.

CURRENT APPROACHES TO IT: SECURITY

One popular approach for risk visualization has been the construction of a risk cube, where each axis or dimension represents one of the three components of risk (threats, assets, and vulnerabilities), and the volume of the cube represents the amount of risk (Loren., 2011) models have been developed which attempt to deal with risk analysis in a qualitative manner.

Current Recent Cyber Security Trends

Devices and Apps

Apps have accelerated the integration of mobile devices within our daily lives. From mapping apps, to social networking, to productivity tools, to games, apps have largely driven the smartphone revolution and have made it as significant and as far-reaching as it is today. While apps demonstrate utility that is seemingly bound only by developer imagination, it also increases the risk of supporting BYOD devices in a corporate environment. This presents mainly two security risks:

- Malicious apps (malware): the increase in the number of apps on the device increases the likelihood that some may contain malicious code or security holes
- App vulnerabilities: apps developed or deployed by the organization to enable access to corporate data may contain security weaknesses

Every new smart phone, tablet or other mobile device, opens another window for a cyber attack as each creates another vulnerable access point to networks. This unfortunate dynamic is no secret to thieves who are ready and waiting with highly targeted malware and attacks employing mobile applications. Similarly, the perennial problem of lost and stolen devices will expand to include these new technologies and old ones that previously flew under the radar of cyber security planning.

Social Media Networking

A social network is a social structure made up of individuals or organizations called nodes, which are connected by one or more specific types of interdependency, such as friendship, common interest, and exchange of finance, relationships of beliefs, knowledge or prestige (Gharibi, Shaabi, 2012).

The popularity of social media is such that worldwide active users of social media are expected to reach around 2.95 billion by 2020, which is about one third of the world's entire population (Clement, 2019). Growing use of social media will contribute to personal cyber threats. Social media adoption among businesses is skyrocketing and so is the threat of attack. In 2012, organizations can expect to see an increase in social media profiles used as a channel for social engineering tactics. To combat the risks, companies will need to look beyond the basics of policy and procedure development to more advanced technologies such as data leakage prevention, enhanced network monitoring and log file analysis. Classic threats have been an issue ever since the development of the Internet. These threats are spam, malware, phishing, or cross-site scripting (XSS) attacks. Modern approaches include clickjacking, de-anonymization attacks, fake profiles, identity clone attacks, inference attacks, information leakage, location leakage, cyberstalking, user profiling, surveillance (Ali et. al, 2018).

Cloud Computing

More firms will use cloud computing. The significant cost savings and efficiencies of cloud computing are compelling companies to migrate to the cloud. A well designed architecture and operational security planning will enable organizations to effectively manage the risks of cloud computing. Unfortunately, current surveys and reports indicate that companies are underestimating the importance of security due diligence when it comes to vetting these providers. As cloud use rises in 2012, new breach incidents will highlight the challenges these services pose to forensic analysis and incident response and the matter of cloud security will finally get its due attention.

Extended Reality

A risk that is specific to augmented reality is a virtual graffiti attack – the use of AR-enhanced Internet of Things devices to virtually deface build-ings, landmarks, signage or other workplace surfaces with negative, unauthorized imagery, and then share with others (Barometer, 2016). A framework to allows stakeholders to reduce a Collaborative Mixed Reality attack surface as well understand how Intrusion Detection System (IDS) approaches can be adopted for CMR systems is presented here (Happa et al., 2019).

Internet of Things

The Internet of Things is the term used to describe the connectivity of electronic smart devices and systems that are able to communicate with each other and share data wirelessly. In 2014, Cisco estimated that some 10 billion devices were wirelessly connected worldwide, and by 2020 Cisco researchers predicted that that number would rise to 50 billion (Evans, 2011).

A device which connects to the Internet, whether it is a constraint or smart device, inherits the security risks of today's computer devices, such as authorization, authentication, confidentiality, trust, and data security need to be considered.

While the IoT is entering daily life more and more, security risks pertaining to IoT are growing and are changing rapidly.

HP study reveals 70% of Internet of Things devices vulnerable to attacks (Rativson, 2014).

Cyber security of IoT in recent years has become a matter of interest for the European Commission and other regulation bodies. In 2015, the European Commission launched the Alliance for Internet of Things Innovation (AIOTI) (EC, 2015) with the objective to create an innovative European IoT ecosystem. It has become the largest IoT association in Europe illustrating the EU's intention to collaborate with stakeholders in order to establish a competitive European IoT market and develop new business models. In the same year, EU adopted the Digital Single Market (DSM) Strategy (EU Commission, 2019)) to address common issues that may lead to the deceleration of secure IoT adoption, such as fragmentation of guidelines and lack of interoperability. In 2017 the US IoT Cybersecurity Improvement Act (United States Congress, 2017) was introduced to address IoT security issues.

Space Cyber Security

Space systems, including ground systems and satellites, are vulnerable to attack. Current cybersecurity mitigation techniques and recommended cybersecurity principles are presented by Falco G. (2018). Falco defines space systems as assets that either exist in suborbital or outer space or ground control systems – including launch facilities, for these assets. Space asset organizations are organizations that build, operate, maintain or own space systems. Critical infrastructure is defined by the US Department of Homeland Security as 16 different sectors that seem discreet; yet, there are many commonalities across them. For example, most critical infrastructure relies on space systems..

Threats to cyber security can be roughly divided into two general categories: actions aimed at and intended to damage or destroy cyber systems (——cyber attacks) and actions that seek to exploit the cyberinfrastructure for unlawful or harmful purposes without damaging or compromising that infrastructure(—— cyber exploitation‖) (Blair, 2009).Common cyber threats include: phishing and spear phishing, malicious code, weak and default passwords, unpatched o outdated software vulnerabilities, removable media. For each of these threats, a description as well as indicators and countermeasures are presented below. The main cybersecurity technical measures are:

Private Measures

Non-governmental entities play major roles in the cyber security arena. Technical standards for the Internet (including current and next-generation versions of the Internet Protocol) are developed and proposed by the privately controlled Internet Engineering Task Force (——IETF‖); the Web Consortium, housed at the Massachusetts Institute of Technology, defines technical standards for the Web. Other privately controlled entities that play significant operational roles on aspects of cyber security include the major telecommunications carriers, Internet Service Providers (——ISPs‖), and many other organizations, including: The Forum of Incident Response and Security Teams (——FIRST‖), The Institute of Electrical and Electronics Engineers (——IEEE‖), The Internet Corporation for Assigned Names and Numbers (——ICANN‖).

National Measures

Many national governments have adopted laws aimed at punishing and thereby deterring specific forms of cyber attacks or exploitation.e.g. NSA, to cooperate with private entities in evaluating the source and nature of cyber attacks.

International Measures

National governments often cooperate with each other informally by exchanging information, investigating attacks or crimes, preventing or stopping harmful conduct, providing evidence, and even arranging for the rendition of individuals to a requesting state. States have also made formal, international agreements that bear directly or indirectly on cyber security (Council of Europe, 2020).

CYBERTERRORISM

The phenomenon of **Cyberterrorism** is becoming more and more dangerous. In fact it is economic, anonymous, it can be carried out at a distance, it has an impressive amount of objectives at its disposal, it makes recruitment easy and fund raising, it can strike, though not always lethally, an extremely large number of objectives and, finally, it is capable of generating much greater coverage on the part of the media, a goal - this - particularly sought after by terrorists (Atlante geopolotico, 2019).

In **target oriented cyberterrorism**, the network is intended as a goal and as a weapon; it consists in attacks or threats of attacks against computers, networks and information stored therein, in order to intimidate or force a government or its population to certain behaviors to achieve political or social effects, or in acts that block or destroy computerized nodes of critical infrastructures such as the internet, telecommunications, electricity networks, the banking system, etc.

In **tool oriented Cyberterrorism,** the network is intended primarily as a tool and as a support. It therefore consists of operations conducted on the Web and politically motivated for the purpose of cause serious consequences, such as loss of life or substantial economic damage, or in any case terror. The network therefore represents a support allowing to carry out all the activities inherent to the management and survival of the terrorist organization, such as propaganda, fundraising, communication, organization and recruitment.

Recent example is the cyberattack during the Russia-Georgia war in 2008 and Estonian in 2011 apparatuses, operated by Russian forces, or the US computer stunt / ex attack against an Iranian power plant in 2014, or, the recent "Anonymous" organization. Their actions range from the suppression of digital services (DDoS) to the dissemination of secret or top-secret material.

The attacks against Georgia's Internet infrastructure began with coordinated barrages of millions of requests — known as distributed denial of service, or D.D.O.S., attacks — that overloaded and effectively shut down Georgian servers. Exactly who was behind the cyberattack is not known. The Georgian government blamed Russia for the attacks, but the Russian government said it was not involved. It was descovered by Jose Nazario of Arbor Networks in Lexington, who noticed a stream of data directed at Georgian government sites containing the message: "win+love+in+Russia."According to Internet technical experts, it was the first time a known cyberattack had coincided with a shooting war (Lomidze, 2011).

- Attack on governmental web resources Damage of reputation
- Shut down media, forums, blogs Georgia People could not get real Information, misinformation of real facts by Russian Media
- Block and cut off Georgian Internet resources Communication was impossible within the country as well as outside.

Types of suffered Cyber Attacks:

- Geographically distributed BOTNETS (300-400 sessions per IP per server
- SQL INJECTION of more than 100 sites (Examples:
- Attempts of BGP hijacking
- Websites hacking (According servers securities levels it can be said that hackers knew passwords)
- Spamming of Email addresses

Cyberattacks are so inexpensive and easy to mount, with few fingerprints, they will almost certainly remain a feature of modern warfare. Every structure connected to the global network is potentially at risk of attack. The change in quality of the threat has involved a reorganization of the Intelligence forces, including an increase in human resources and analytical technologies. Not being a limited physical space and of the finite, the criminal action can be performed from any location located anywhere and from a great distance, in a protected anonymity. If the defensive tools increase, the capacity for offense increases, with the difference that the former are studied and produced in response to the latter, therefore within a context of predictability, while the latter act in search of increasingly new and powerful means, thus playing also on the unpredictability.

In 2008 Creating CERT.GE (Based on GRENA) and in 2011 CERT.GOV. GE (Based on DEA). Specifically,

- **CERT Web Portal** (Computer Incident Reporting Portal): Created for farther analyzing and responding. It supports ticket system for registered users. www.dea.gov.ge
- **Incident Handling:** Dedicated to identifying Security Incidents and helping to solve it.
- **Penetration Test Service**: For Public Sector for analyzing cyber resources for the vulnerabilities and reporting them.
- **Governmental Organization**: Starting to care about Cyber threats .

- **Big Commercial Organizations**: Collaborating with Government in Cyber Security Filed.

In April 2007, the Estonian Government moved a memorial commemorating the Soviet liberation of the country from the Nazis to a less prominent and visible location in Tallinn. This decision triggered rioting among Russian-speaking minorities and cyber terrorism targeting Estonia's critical economic and political infrastructure (Herzog, 2011).

Estonia and Russia have a long history of strife in their bilateral relationship, and the problems between these ethnic populations date back to hundreds of years before the existence of modern nation-states. Following the Soviet annexation of the Baltic States in 1940, and throughout the Cold War, the Kremlin relocated hundreds of thousands of ethnic Russians to Estonia. The purpose behind these mass migrations was two-fold: to increase cohesion in the Eastern Bloc and to "Russify" Estonian culture. Following the end of the Cold War and the dissolution of the U.S.S.R., the government in Tallinn implemented policies designed to minimize Russian influences on Estonian culture (Smith, 2003. Lauristin&Heidmets, 2002).

The 2007 cyber terrorism on Estonia was more than just a temporary nuisance; rather, it was a mild version of a new form of digital violence that could halt public services, commerce, and government operations. Estonian Defense Minister Jaak Aaviksoo observed that successful cyberattacks can effectively be compared to when your ports are shut to the sea (Ruus, 2008).

A blockade is a fitting analogy, as future cyber-terrorist attacks may disrupt a country's water and electricity supplies, telecommunications (severing its connections to the world), and national defenses. The seriousness of the attacks on Estonia generated a rapid international response. Estonia had few formal cyber-defense preparations outside of its framework for countering traditional acts of terrorism (Sieber&Brunst, 2007) and the government Computer Emergency Response Team (CERT) required Finnish, German, Israeli, and Slovenian assistance to restore normal network operations.31 NATO CERTs provided additional assistance, while the EU's European Network and Information Security Agency (ENISA) offered expert technical assessments of the developing situation. Further, a high level of intelligence sharing took place among western countries during the crisis.

In this period of IT-driven globalization, the attacks on Estonia demonstrate that even NATO Article 5 and U.S. nuclear umbrella guarantees cannot ensure the protection of a nationstate's sovereignty in cyberspace.

Figure 2. Concepts cloud

CYBERINTELLIGENCE AND COUNTERINTELLIGENCE

Intelligence is increasingly facilitating information superiority through an understanding of the cyber domain. According to the United States Department of Defence, cyber intelligence is:

1. The product resulting from the collection, processing, integration, evaluation, analysis, and interpretation of available information concerning foreign nations, hostile or potentially hostile forces or elements, or areas of actual or potential operations.
2. The activities that result in the product.
3. The organisations engaged in such activities.

The process for developing effective cyber intelligence strategies relies on the steps mentioned above that "result in the product", those being the "collection, processing, integration, evaluation, analysis, and interpretation" of relevant data and information. Essentially, these steps represent the cycle of cyber intelligence (Kahalani, 2019).

Counter-Intelligence is a phase of intelligence covering the activity devoted in destroying the effectiveness of hostile foreign activities and the protection of information against espionage, subversion and sabotage. Its purposes are:

- The protection of information against espionage
- The protection of personnel against subversion
- The protection of installations and materials against sabotage

to reduce the risk of a failure in a command, increasing its security, to aid in achieving surprise attacks, and to decrease the enemy ability to create information about the forces.

The main categories of Counter-Intelligence Operations are:

1. **Military Security**: It encompasses the measures taken by a command to protect itself against espionage, enemy operation, sabotage, subversion or surprise
2. **Port boundary and Travel Security**: It has to do with the application of both military and civil security measures for counterintelligence control at point of entry and departure, international borders and boundaries
3. **Civil Security:** It encompasses active and passive counterintelligence measures affecting the non-military nationals permanently or temporarily residing in an area under military jurisdiction.
4. **Special Operations:** It concerns the counter subversion, sabotage and espionage

States are behaving rationally in cyberspace. The rational behavior of states provides a substantial framework upon which to build future models for deterrence as well as within which to predict state actions in cyberspace (Brantly, 2016). There is a growing societal and military reliance on all things cyber, often difficult to see.

In USA, a new operational component was added to the existing four Agency's Directorates (Directorate of Operations, Directorate of Analysis, Directorate of Science and Technology, Directorate of Support): the Directorate of Digital Innovation (DDI). The Directorate of Digital Innovation focused on accelerating innovation across the Agency's mission activities with cutting-edge digital and cyber tradecraft and IT infrastructure, in support of the CIA's clandestine and open source intelligence collection missions.

When a state decides to attack another state, there are two fundamental aspects in application into the cyber domain (Brantly, 2016):

- it is not concerned solely with its relative power to its adversary. but with the power of its adversary
- it is concerned with its ability to conduct an attack against an adversary while maintaining anonymity.

Anonymity in cyberspace in the initiation and implementation phases of an attack provides the freedom to maneuver. It means a "power", a fundamental concept that underpins international relations theory,largely absent from many discussions on cyberspace. The "power" plays a role in influencing state actions or the actions of individuals.

Brantly builds a rationalist argument. By establishing a decision-making framework it is possible to examine why and when covert actions (such as OCOs) are employed. The lines between decision and action are drawn out. Offensive Cyber Operations (OCOs) by state actors are a new typology of covert action. The analysis proceeds in sections each adding to the case that OCOs by states are a form of covert action. Brantly points out that the U.S. government's approach to cyberspace has to this point relied on the military, with Admiral Mike Rogers currently the commander of both the National Security Agency and Cyber Command (CYBERCOM). The president has given the military, and not the Central Intelligence Agency (CIA), the lead as the main covert operator in the cyber domain.

The Department of Defense's "Joint Vision 2020" establishes the goal of information superiority on the battlefield. This information superiority enables decision superiority and favorably tilts the strategic and tactical balance. Information superiority is built on cyber power scale and complexity of attacks, robustness of defense, policy positions, systemic vulnerabilities and dependencies, actor anonymity and attribution issues.

To explain the foundations for why states engage in cyber attacks, Brantly focus on a rational choice approach to the decision-making process and honing the decision process using expected utility.

Table 1. The U.S. international strategy for cyberspace (Freely retrieved from: https://2009-2017.state.gov/documents/organization/255014.pdf)

GOALS	DESCRIPTION
Promote Norms and Build International Security	Build global consensus regarding responsible state behavior in cyberspace including the application of existing international law to enhance stability, ground national security policies, strengthen partnerships, and prevent misinterpretations that can lead to conflict
Fight Cybercrime	Enhance states' ability to fight cybercrime, including promoting international cooperation and information sharing, training for law enforcement, forensic specialists, jurists, and legislators
Strengthen Internet Public Policy and Internet Governance	Develop policies that promote international standards and innovation; enhance security, reliability, and resiliency; extend collaboration and the rule of law; promote inclusive Internet governance structures and institutions that include stakeholders from government, civil society, and the private sector and effectively serve the needs of all internet users
Support Internet Freedom	Preserve and expand the Internet as an open, global space for free expression; organize and interaction across the full range of human interests and endeavors, promote international consensus on the application of human rights in cyberspace; provide political and technical support for individuals facing internet repression; encourage companies to adopt practices and policies that respect human rights online
Perform Cybersecurity Due Diligence	Develop and strengthen relationships with other countries to improve global cybersecurity by enhancing domestic network defense, and incident management and recovery capabilities; increasing participation in existing regional and global cybersecurity structures; cooperating in efforts to address threats of mutual concern
Develop the Internet and Information and Communication Technologies (ICTs) for Economic Growth	Expand ICT infrastructure; increase access to the Internet; encourage the production of appealing and contextually relevant online content for local users as a means of catalyzing economic and social development

INFORMATION WARFARE

Information warfare is any action to deny, exploit, corrupt, or destroy the enemy's information and its functions, protecting ourselves against those actions, and - exploiting our own military information functions. Information Operations are actions taken to affect adversary information and information systems while defending one's own information and information system. For centuries, **cryptography** has been used to conceal and reveal messages.

The traditional forms of Information Warfare are Psychological Operations, Electronic Warfare, Physical Destruction, Security Measures - Deception, Information Attack.

Psychological operations use information to affect the enemy's reasoning. "We can be sure that the global battlefield of the 21st century will be over information -- the dissemination or withholding of facts, the interpretation of events, the presentation or distortion of ideas and ideologies, and the communication of messages and symbols carefully prepared to provoke a particular reaction, either conscious or unconscious, from a target audience."(Africa 2000's website). Global info-sphere is influenced by events and information from the battlefield ('space').

Figure 3. Electronic warfare's types
(Source: https://defence.pk/pdf/threads/electronic-warfare-an-indispensable-aspect-of-modern-war.423987/

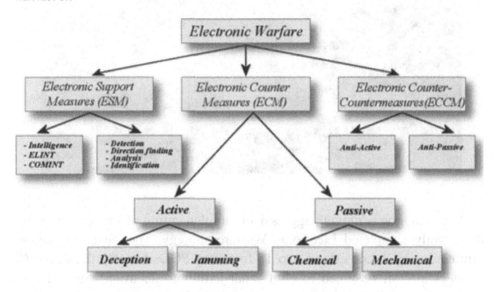

Electronic Warfare denies accurate information to the enemy to determine, exploit, reduce, or prevent hostile use of the electromagnetic spectrum. It includes: electronic countermeasures, electronic counter-countermeasures, electronic warfare support measures (Jiindals, 2016).

Countries which have understood the importance of EW and thereby electronic countermeasures and counter-countermeasures will try to maintain its quick evolution, since electronic warfare is progressively poised to become the primary means of warfare to gain advantage over the enemy in a war scenario whereby its usage will facilitate in gaining impunity for unopposed assault or substantially diminish the resistance of the adversary. Improving electronic warfare modeling and simulation to better prepare for emerging weapons systems is also a key element of the strategy. This can help anticipate or train against future weapons threats which may not exist yet but nevertheless pose an emerging threat.

Figure 4. Electronic Warfare. An example
(Source: http://www.asdnews.com/news/defense/2019/04/10/electronic-warfare-market-set-grow-36bn-2029

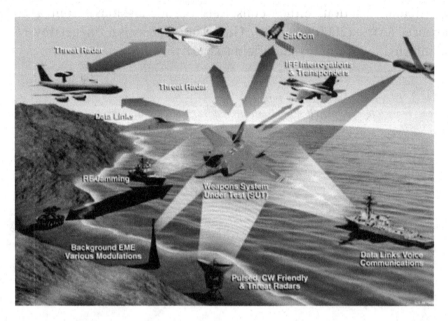

The Pentagon is moving aggressively implementing major provisions of its recently completed Electronic Warfare strategy. The Next-Generation Jammer, or NGJ, consists of two 15-foot long PODs beneath the EA-18G Growler aircraft designed to emit radar-jamming electronic signals; one jammer goes on each side of the aircraft.The NGJ departs from existing EW systems in that it can jam multiple frequencies at one time, increasing the scope and effectiveness of attacks. This better enables U.S. aircraft to elude or "jam" more Russian-built air defenses able to detect aircraft on a wide range of frequencies, such as X-band, VHF and UHF. Russian-built S-300 and S-400 air defenses are believed to be among the best in the world.Radar technology sends an electromagnetic ping forward, bouncing it off objects before analyzing the return signal to determine a target's location, size, shape and speed. However, if the electromagnetic signal is interfered with, thwarted or "jammed" in some way, the system is then unable to detect the objects, or targets (Osborn, 2018).

All warfare is based on **deception.** Hence, "when we are able to attack, we must seem unable; when using our forces, we must seem inactive; when we are near, we must make the enemy believe we are far away; when far away, we must make him believe we are near" (Taylor, 2019).

EXAMPLES OF INFORMATION WARFARE

Zapatista Information Strike (Socialnetwar)

In January 1994, a guerrilla-like insurgency begun in Chiapas by the Zapatista National Liberation Army (EZLN), and the Mexican government's response to it, aroused a multitude of civilsociety activists associated with a variety of nongovernmental organizations (NGOs) to "swarm, electronically as well as physically, from the United States, Canada, and elsewhere into Mexico City and Chiapas. At present, neither social (EZLN/Zapatista), guerrilla (EPR), or criminal (drug-trafficking) netwar actors seem likely to make Mexico ungovernable, or to create a situation that leads to a newly authoritarian regime. This might occur, if these netwars all got interlaced and reinforced each other, directly or indirectly, under conditions where an economic recession deepens, the federal government and the PRI (presumably still in power) lose legitimacy to an alarming degree, and infighting puts the elite "revolutionary family" and its political clans into chaos (Ronfeldt &Arquilla, 1998).

India/Pakistan Kashmir Cyber Conflict

The regional rivalry between India and Pakistan has existed since the two nations achieved independence in the Partition of India. Their relationship is characterized by fierce military and economic competition, resulting in small-scale skirmishes, war, and provocation in the physical and cyber realms.

The actors involved in India and Pakistan's cyber rivalry thus far are primarily hacktivists and patriotic hackers from both states. They targeted both government websites and poorly protected non-governmental websites with website defacement. Technologically, much of the cyber-activities observed in the India-Pakistan rivalry showed that even with relatively unsophisticated cybertools, both APTs managed to steal information and achieve their strategic goals (Baezner, 2018).

Stuxnet Device-Control Strike

Iran's nuclear programme has been threatened by a powerful virus distributed through the internet. The problem started on a Vancouver stage in 2010, where a young Irish computing expert gave a filmed presentation showing how the world could end with the pop of a balloon. He was demonstrating how a computer worm called Stuxnet had effects that went beyond blowing up your computer screen. Stuxnet has infected operating systems on equipment manufactured by the German industrial giant Siemens and has, as he put it, *"real-world implications beyond any threat we have seen in the past"*. It could attack oil pipelines, power stations, even nuclear plants (Spencer, 2010).

CONCLUSION

The information revolution is leading to the rise of network forms of organization, whereby small, previously isolated groups can communicate, link up, and conduct coordinated joint actions as never before. Although many market sectors obtained benefits from these new technologies, the necessity of security concerns increased. Bailenson (2018) highlight privacy issues of users nonverbal data (eye movements, facial expressions, body movements etc.) collected by companies during extended reality experiences in order to further improve applications based on users behavior. These data are also shared by companies with a number of associated affiliates. Many virtual reality headsets, like Oculus Rift and HTC Vive Pro, are currently available on the market at consumer level. These headsets are often connected to online transactions which use personal and financial data. Geo-tacking information are tracked by many augmented reality apps, like Pokémon Go.

REFERENCES

AA.VV. (2008). Cyber Security Strategy. *Estonian Ministry of Defense*. Available at: www.mod.gov.ee/files/kmin/img/files/ Kuberjulgeoleku_strateegia_2008-2013_ENG.pdf

Ali, S., Islam, N., Rauf, A., Din, I., Guizani, M., & Rodrigues, J. (2018). Privacy and Security Issues in Online Social Networks. *Future Internet*, *2018*(10), 114. doi:10.3390/fi10120114

Atlante Geopolitico. (2019). *Cyberterrorism*. Retrieved in http://www.treccani.it/enciclopedia/cyberterrorismo_(Atlante-Geopolitico)/

Baezner M. (2018). *Regional rivalry between IndiaPakistan: tit-for-tat in cyberspace*. Center for Security Studies (CSS), ETH Zürich.

Bailenson, J. N. (2018). Protecting Nonverbal Data Tracked in Virtual Reality. *JAMA Pediatrics, 172*(10), 905. doi:10.1001/jamapediatrics.2018.1909 PMID:30083770

Barometer R. (2016). Risks And Rewards Of Adding Augmented Reality To Connected Device. *ISACA 2016 IT RISK.*

Blair, D. C. (2009). *Annual Threat Assessment.* House Permanent Select Committee on Intelligence, 111th Congress, 1st sess.

Brantly, A. (2016). *The decision to attack. Military and Intelligence Cyber Decision-making.* Studies in Security and International Affairs.

Clement, J. (2019). *Social Media Statistics & Facts.* Available in: https://www.statista.com/topics/1164/social-networks/

Council of Europe. (2020). *Convention on Cybercrime CETS No. 185.* http://conventions.coe.int/Treaty/Commun/ChercheSig. asp?NT=185&CM=1&DF=&CL=ENG

David Ronfeldt John Arquilla. (1998). *The zapatista "social netwar" in Mexico.* RAND by the United States Army.

EC European Commission. (2015). *The Alliance for Internet of Things Innovation.* Retrieved from: https://ec.europa.eu/digital-single-market/en/alliance-internet-things-innovation-aioti

EU Commission. (2019). *Empowering people with new generation technology, Policy 2019-2024.* retrieved in: https://ec.europa.eu/info/priorities/europe-fit-digital-age_en

Evans, D. (2011). *The Internet of Things How the Next Evolution of the Internet Is Changing Everything. Cisco Internet Business Solutions Group.* IBSG.

Falco, G. (2018). The Vacuum of Space Cybersecurity. AIAA SPACE and Astronautics Forum and Exposition, Orlando, FL.

Gharibi, W., & Shaabi, M. (2012). Cyber Threats In Social Networking Websites. *International Journal of Distributed and Parallel Systems, 3*(1). Available at: https://arxiv.org/pdf/1202.2420.pdf

Gibson, W. (1984). *Neuromancer.* Ace Science Fiction Specials, Ace Books.

Gibson, W. (1989). *Cyberspace. In Interview* (p. 128). New York: Berkley Publishing Group.

Happa J. (2019). Cyber Security Threats and Challenges in Collaborative Mixed-Reality. *Front. ICT*.

Herzog, S. (2011). Revisiting the Estonian Cyber Attacks: Digital Threats and Multinational Responses. *Journal of Strategic Security, 4*(2).

Janczewski, L., & Colarik, A. (2008). Cyber warfare and cyber terrorism. Information Science Reference.

Jindals, S. (2016). *Electronic Warfare: An Indispensable Aspect Of Modern War*. Discussion in 'Indian Defence Forum' 2016.

Kahalani, A. (2019). *What is Cyber Intelligence?* Retrieved from. https://www.blackhawkintelligence.com/what-is-cyber-intelligence/

Lauristin, M., & Heidmets, M. (Eds.). (2002). *The Challenge of the Russian Minority: Emerging Multicultural Democracy in Estonia*. Tartu: Tartu University Press.

Lomidze, I. (2011). Cyber Attack against Georgia. *GITI 2011*. Retrieved from: https://dea.gov.ge/uploads/GITI%202011/GITI2011_3.pdf

Loren. (2011). Decision support for Cyber security risk planning. Decision Support Systems 2011.

Osborn, K. (2018). *Pentagon Moves on New Electronic Warfare Strategy & Weapons*. Available in: https://defensemaven.io/warriormaven/future-weapons/pentagon-moves-on-new-electronic-warfare-strategy-weapons-4NHRKk8t506S4FI3HhOifQ/

Rawlinson, K. (2014). HP Study Reveals 70 Percent of Internet of Things Devices Vulnerable to Attack. *Hp website*. Available in: https://www8.hp.com/us/en/hp-news/press-release.html?id=1744676

Ruus, K. (2008). Cyber War I: Estonia Attacked from Russia. *European Affairs, 9*, 1.

Sieber, U., Phillip, W., & Brunst, P. W. (2007). *Cyberterrorism—the use of the Internet for terrorist purposes*. Strasbourg: Council of Europe Publishing.

Smith, D. J. (2003). Minority Rights, Multiculturalism and EU Enlargement: The Case of Estonia. *Journal on Ethnopolitics and Minority Rights Issues in Europe, 4*(1), 22-23.

Spencer, R. (2010). Stuxnet virus attack on Iranian nuclear programme: the first strike by computer? *The Telegraph Journal*. Retrieved from: https://www.telegraph.co.uk/news/worldnews/middleeast/iran/8040656/Stuxnet-virus-attack-on-Iranian-nuclear-programme-the-first-strike-by-computer.html

Taylor, P. (2019). *From Information Warfare to Information Operation to the global war on terrorism*. Lecture 4, ICS, University of Leeds. Available in: https://slideplayer.com/slide/16461516/

Tonellotto, M. (2014). Evidenza informatica, computer forensics e best practices. Rivista di Criminologia, Vittimologia e Sicurezza, 8(2).

Tonge, A., Kasture, S. S., & Chaudhari, S. (2013). Cyber Security: challenges for society – literature review. *IOSR Journal of Computer Engineering*, *12*(2), 67-75. https://pdfs.semanticscholar.org/61fd/814aae913ed3f0ab6459625ffc6944952757.pdf?_ga=2.84089305.199330368.1560936122-811949187.1560936122

United State Congress. (2017). *Internet of Things (IoT) Cybersecurity Improvement Act of 2017*. Retrieved in: https://www.congress.gov/bill/115th-congress/senate-bill/1691/text?format=txt

KEY TERMS AND DEFINITIONS

Cyber Warfares: They are all those activities aimed at causing damage to computer systems of any kind. Unlike "normal" cyber-attacks, these are actions carried out with specific political-military purposes by special military apparatus or by cyber-criminal organizations financed, in any case, by government entities.

Information Warfare: It is a concept involving the battlespace use and management of information and communication technology (ICT) in pursuit of a competitive advantage over an opponent (Wikipedia). It is an emerging asymmetric threat that forces us to innovate our security approach.

Chapter 8
Using Extended Reality to Support Cyber Security

ABSTRACT

Cyber security is a constantly evolving area of interest. Many solutions are currently available and new methods and technologies are emerging. Although some solutions already exist in extended reality, a lack of engagement and storytelling is available, with a consequence of decreasing the probability of dissemination and awareness of the risks involved in cybersecurity. This chapter gives an overview of an extended reality platform that can be potentially used for the simulation of security threats and that combines artificial intelligence and game design principles. The main goal of this research is to develop an extended reality solution to simulate a story involving virtual characters and objects for the entertainment industry, with possible applications in other sectors such as education and training. After an introduction to extended reality, the chapter focuses on an overview on the available extended reality technologies in the context of cybersecurity.

INTRODUCTION

Extended Reality is a term referring to all real and virtual combined environments and human-machine interactions generated by computer technology and wearables. It includes new technologies such as virtual reality, augmented reality and mixed reality. This term includes not only real and virtual combined environments, but also human-machine interactions

DOI: 10.4018/978-1-7998-1562-4.ch008

generated by computer technology and wearables (Berglund, 2008). The rise of these technologies introduced new possibilities in many market sectors, from education and training to cyber intelligence, cyber security, and situation of awareness.

STATE OF THE ART

Researchers have explored this area since the 1960s (Sutherland, 1968). However, it is only recently that Extended Reality have begun shipping commercially. Augmented Reality is nowadays available at consumer level, with applications downloadable through Google Play and Apple Store. Examples include Pokémon Go, Word Lens and Porsche AR application. Microsoft released a Mixed Reality headset called HoloLens, Apple released an augmented reality glasses called Google Glass, Vive released HTC Vive Pro. There are already around 111,000 AR headsets in operation in the commercial segment and projected more than 20 million by 2021 .

The global mixed reality market is expected to record a CAGR of about 70.20%, over the forecast period of 2018-2023 (Research and Markets, 2018).

The most intuitive definition of augmented reality was given in 1994 by Paul Milgram and Fumio Kishino (Milgram, 1994), professors of University of Toronto and University of Osaka, respectively.

Milgram and Kishino described a taxonomy, the *Reality-Virtual Continuum*, which explains how Augmented Reality and Virtual Reality are linked together (see Figure1).

Figure 1. Reality-Virtuality (RV) Continuum (Milgram, 1994)

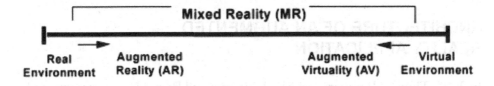

Reality-Virtuality (RV) Continuum

According to Milgram, the real world and the virtual environment represents two extreme conditions, graphically illustrated in the *Milgram scale*. Among these extreme conditions, there is the continuum between real and virtual environments, where virtual and real components are present. In this scale, augmented reality is on the left, near the real environment, because of the predominance of the real environment compared to the virtual elements.

In order to have a clear understanding of the terms involved in the Reality-Virtuality Continuum, please take a look at the Figure2, Figure3, and Figure4.

- **Real Environment:** Is the environment seen by the observer (no virtual elements are shown)
- **Augmented Reality:** is the surrounding real environment in which virtual elements are shown in overlay
- **Augmented Virtuality**: is a virtual environment in which some elements of the real environment are present
- **Virtual Reality**: is a completely virtual environment (no elements from the real worlds are shown)

Figure 2. Virtual Reality driving experience

ARCHITECTURE OF AN AUGMENTED REALITY APPLICATION

In 2004, Thomas Reicher, Asa MacWilliams and Bernd Brügges identified a common architecture to all augmented reality applications (Reicher, 2004). This architecture is subdivided in six parts (see Figure 5):

- **Application Subsystem**: is the code container of the entire application
- **Interaction Subsystem:** collect and process user inputs

Figure 3. Augmented Reality application for Intern Design

Figure 4. Mixed Reality application for Architecture

- **Presentation Subsystem:** visualize outputs (contents)
- **Tracking Subsystem**: track user position and share results with other subsystems
- **Context Subsystem**: collect non-tracking data and share them with other subsystems
- **World Model Subsystem:** stores information related to the user behaviour in the real world

These subsystems are subdivided into several components, as shown in the picture below (Figure 5).

Figure 5. UML graph showing the architecture of an AR application

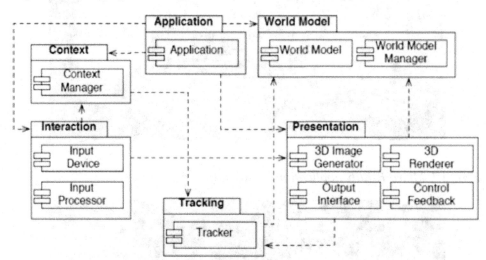

Virtual reality and Augmented Reality aim to give to the user an immersive experience using different methodologies, respectively. Intuitively, virtual reality let the user see virtual elements in a virtual environment. Augmented reality, instead, let the user see virtual elements in a real environment.

In virtual reality, the user is immersed in a virtual environment (e.g. the user is wearing a virtual reality headset) and can explore the environment moving the head in each direction (vertically, horizontally) and walking within the environment (e.g. through controllers with directional buttons). Furthermore, the user has a clear perception of himself in the virtual environment and of the distance between himself and the virtual elements available in the virtual environment.

Augmented Reality, instead, increase the user's visual perception of the physical space with virtual elements (images, models, text, etc.). The resulting experience is a blend between real world and virtual elements, as a whole, enabling the user to see and possibly interact with the virtual elements. Therefore, the challenge is to give a perception that the real world and the virtual world are blended as one thing.

A LITTLE BIT OF HISTORY

Sensorama

The birth of augmented reality can be considered as early as 50s.

Morton Heilig can be considered the precursor of augmented reality. At the end of 50s, Morton Heilig invented a simulator called Sensorama, with the goal of extend cinema and human senses (see Figure6). This device enabled to see five movies, with sounds and smells (e.g. the wind created from the orientation of the machine).

Figure 6. Sensorama

 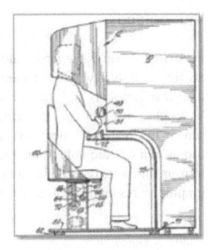

Human Mounted Display (HMD)

In 1968, Ivan Sutherland, professor at Harvard University, together with his student Bob Sproull, created the first real augmented reality system, called Human Mounted Display (HMD). This devices was a viewer device to wear on the head, like an helmet, with a little optical display on the front of one or both eyes (called "Sword of Damocles), as shown in Figure7.

Figure 7. La spada di Damocle

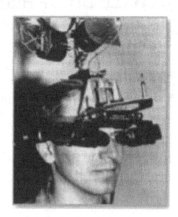

Videoplace

In 1975, Myron Krueger created *Videoplace,* a device able to create an artificial reality in which users are immersed. This system was able to respond to user movements and actions, without the need to wear glasses of gloves. Videoplace used projectors, cameras, hardware, and special effects on the screen to create an interactive environment. Users, located in separated rooms in a lab, are able to interact together through this technology. Users' movements were recorded in a video, analyzed and then transferred through graphic representations to other users in the same environment (see Figure 8).

Figure 8. Videoplace

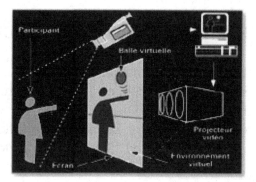

Head Mounted Display by Tom Caudell

In 1990 Tom Caudell, a former researcher at Boeing, introduced for the first time the term Augmented Reality to describe a digital display used by technicians of aircrafts that blend virtual graphs with the real world. He and colleague David Mizell were asked to come up with an alternative to the expensive diagrams and marking devices then used to guide workers on the factory floor. They came up with the idea of replacing the large plywood boards, which contained individually designed wiring instructions for each plane, with a head-mounted apparatus that would display a plane's specific schematics through high-tech eyeware and project them onto reusable boards. The proposed head mounted display was monocular and semi-transparent (see Figure 9)

Figure 9. Modifica dell'HMD

KARMA

In 1992 Steven Feiner, Blair MacIntyre and Doree Seligmann presented one of the main articles related to a prototype of Augmented Reality system, called KARMA (see Figure 10), at the Graphics Interface Conference (Feiner, 1993).

Figure 10. KARMA

Theater Production

In 1994 Julie Martin created the Augmented Reality Theater production, the first theatre company in which dancers and acrobats worked together inside a virtual world, interacting with it.

Touring Machine

In 1997 Feiner and his collaborators developed the Touring Machine at Columbia University (Feiner, 1997). This machine shows the user in the real world with virtual information shown in overlay to real world objects the user was watching (see Figure 11). For example, information about buildings, roads, and historical informations.

Figure 11. Touring Machine

ARToolkit

In 199 professor Hirokazu Kato of Nara Institute of Science and Technology, released a software library called ARTooklit. This software library combined video tracking systems, interactions layers, virtual information and 3d graphics and gave the possibility to the community of developers to start exploring the possibilities of augmented reality. This library was leading the way of AR browsers (see Figure 12)

Figure 12. ARToolkit

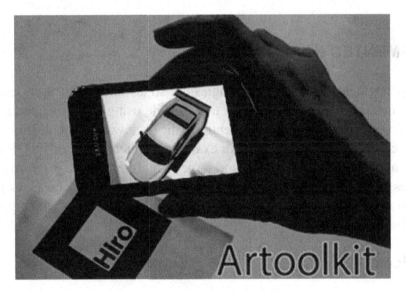

Digital Hologram

In 2009 a substantial change occurred. The usage of AR technology in advertisement leaded to an increased popularity of this technology: during the final of the American Superbow, an advertisement of the planning of electrical networks by General Electrics has been broadcasted. This advertisement also gave a reference of a website in which users can try the experience Digital Hologram (see Figure 13).

Figure 13. Digital Hologram

AUGMENTED REALITY TODAY

Today, augmented reality technologies are so advanced that users can use the camera of their smartphone or tablet while using an augmented reality application. This means that augmented reality is nowadays at consumer level and everyone can experience it. For example, application based on QRcodes let the user scan a particular code and some virtual elements (e.g. information, images or models) are visualized. Most known brands are nowadays using AR to explore all commercial possibilities this technology is bringing to their business.

Devices

Devices like *Oculus Rift* and *HTC Vive* are popular virtual reality headsets nowadays available. AR devices includes tablet, smartphones or headsets with transparent or semi-transparent lenses (e.g. Google Glass, Epson Moverio), as shown in Figure14, but also smartwatches.

Head-up Display

The first uses of augmented reality were military applications: in the early 60s aircrafts and helicopters included the famous head-up display (HUD), a technology that overlays vectorial images to the view of the real world. This technology was used by pilots, as shown in Figure14). This technology has been then integrated on soldiers helmet (Helmet-Mounted Sights or HMS), giving information about missions and paths, and overlaying information about pointing devices of weapons.

Recently, these technologies has been transferred from industry to consumer level. Currently, one of the major uses of augmented reality is in the automotive industry: HUD are embedded in vehicles to display info about the travel and the vehicle itself, in order to avoid any external distraction of the user during the travel. An example is *Navigate Hud SPX-HUD01* of *Pioneer*.

Figure 14. HUD in automotive context (Navgate Hud)

 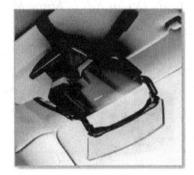

Smartwatches

The term *smartwatch* is commonly used to refer to smart wearable devices like watches. These devices can be connected to smartphones in order to have more features, and can be used to listen music, connect to internet, visualize messages and emails, or call someone. An example is Apple Watch (see Figure 15).

Figure 15. Apple Watch

AR Glasses

Augmented Reality glasses are wearable devices that can be used as glasses and that offers a number of features such as websites browsing, social network access, maps display, GPS positioning, photoshooting and sharing. Examples are Hololens (Microsoft), Google Glass (Google), Vuzix M 100 (Rochester Vuzix), Epson Moverio BT-200 (Epson), Sony SmartEyeglass (Sony). See Figure 16.

Figure 16. Ocular Rift vs Epson Moverio

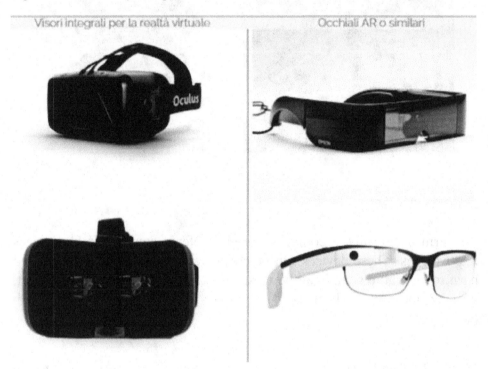

Mobile Devices

The increasing technologic progress in the field of wearable devices leaded to the popularity of augmented reality on those devices: portability, high performant processors, features and apps of wearable devices makes them the main tool for new technologies (see Figure17). An example of AR application available on mobile devices is *Layar* (Figure17).

Figure 17. AR with smartphones

EXTENDED REALITY AND SECURITY

Extended Reality technology is increasingly in demand, predominantly in the media and entertainment industry, but also in other sectors including education, professional training and security. In 2017, Microsoft partnered with the U.S. military to use HoloLens to create wargame scenarios and provide soldiers with battlefield insights via AR simulations. Other military partnerships include ones with the Israeli military and Royal Australian Air Force, both of which studied how HoloLens could be used for planning and training (The Verge, 2019). HoloLens is meant to support the military's goals to improve close-combat effectiveness and survivability across the six following domains: sensing, communication, maneuvering, attack, survival, sustainability (see Figure18).

Carnegie Mellon University researchers developed an augmented reality solution to help soldiers identify and exploit cyber opportunities in the physical environment (Hammerstein, 2017). This project, called Cyber Affordance Visualization in Augmented Reality (CAVIAR), uses Microsoft HoloLens device to dynamically visualize cyber terrain within the user's immediate surroundings (see Figure19).

Augmented Reality can be used to help teenagers to be aware of the risks associated with social networks and always-connected mobile devices, giving shape and form to cybersecurity concepts and allowing students to consolidate them through interactivity (Salazar, 2013).

Figure 18. HoloLens used in military training

Figure 19. CAVIAR project

Emerging extended reality simulators are rapidly become more and more popular. This is due to the possibility of simulation-based learning to allows interactive experiential learning under real environment.

The author of this chapter worked on a H2020 project, called target, that used Mixed Reality and Virtual Reality for Security Critical Agents training (Munro, 2017). This project, aimed to train policemen at operational, tactical and strategic command levels with scenarios that include tactical firearms events, asset protection, mass demonstrations, cyber-attacks and CBRN (Chemical, Biological, Radiological, Nuclear) incidents. More details about the main challenges of the project are discussed in the following section.

CHALLENGES

Cyber Security awareness is a relevant topic and the usage of extended reality simulators can bring the user to virtually experience a cyber attack .

When it comes to extended reality simulators, in particular those that uses virtual characters, a huge amount of field of interest are involved and many processes are required to be undertaken from the design to the development and release. These includes extended reality development, the creation of character animations through motion capture, the creation of 3D models such as virtual characters and objects through 3D modeling, the management of all data retrieved or stored during the experience, the user experience.

Extended Reality technologies has a huge potential and the adoption is constantly growing. However, some challenges and limitations are available as well. According to the device used (e.g. virtual reality headset, smartphone or mixed reality headset), some challenges are involved.

Virtual reality offers the possibility to represents the whole virtual world without problems of limited field of view or distractions by the surrounding environment and with a higher probability of engagement, but some people might feel uncomfortable and in some cases sick due to the difference in movement between the simulated world and the real world. Also, virtual reality has poor results in context in which the user needs to see the real environment (e.g. in the case of training a policemen to use real existing weapons against a virtual human that plays the role of an offender).

Augmented Reality is nowadays available on both headsets and smartphones, and currently offers the possibility to augment virtual contents such as virtual humans, objects or information in overlay on the real world. These possibility open up several possible applications, like the above policemen training but also the augmentation of selected information from a huge amount of data (e.g. showing the calculated probability to be hacked when the user connect the device to a particular network), but it lacks in a real positioning of the virtual contents (the virtual contents are positioned in overlay and not really anchored to the real environment) and also present some challenging difficulties when it comes to storytelling (e.g. how do you represent an environment in which a story take place and at the same time see the real environment surrounding you? How do you create a story that involves both the real environment and the virtual objects?).

Another challenge involved is related about how to engage the user into an experience in which some distractions can be created by the real world (as mentioned above, in augmented reality the user see both virtual contents and real world). Also, available headsets and smartphones have a limited field of view in which the virtual contents are rendered, that increase a risk of the user to miss part of the story (e.g. a virtual object is in the scenario but out of the field of view and therefore not seen by the user).

Mixed Reality anchor virtual objects on the real world, therefore it does not present the problem of the realism that augmented reality has (e.g. with HoloLens headset, the user can see a virtual human positioned exactly on the floor and not floating in the air), but share the same challenges of Augmented Reality when it comes to the field of view and the storytelling representation.

RELATED WORK

Although many solutions are already available, these simulators seem to lack in engagement and few attention has been given to the integration of artificial intelligence to facilitate tasks. This project aims to investigate these aspects, in particular to reach an understanding of what are the possibilities offered by artificial intelligence to propose content according to the profile of the user, and to simulate a story that goes beyond the simple sequence of actions and that can engage the user effectively. The extended reality platform can simulate a story involving virtual characters and objects for the entertainment industry (Gironacci, 2019).

A set of stories are available and pre-configured, and the software solution can suggest to the user which story (or scenario) to load (see Figure 20).

Figure 20. XRTS simulator

RESEARCH METHODOLOGY

Several investigations has also been performed before the development of the development of the simulator. These includes:

- Showcasing previous investigation performed in the Extended Reality field
- Evaluation of Extended Reality (XR) devices currently available
- Exploration of Extended Reality (XR) software libraries currently available
- Exploration of Artificial Intelligence software libraries
- Exploration of Motion Capture options
- Exploration of further technologies that could be potentially used for this project
- Development of basic example with the above devices, software libraries and other technologies to have a comprehensive understanding of their possibilities and limitations.
- Development of the extended reality solution

Design of the System

The system is composed by three components: a database to store data such as user profiles and settings, a backend to make those data accessible by the front-end and to handle core computations, and a front-end application that can run on an extended reality headset.

Modules

The proposed solution is composed by several modules: a core module for both logics and common processes, a login module to login as a user in the front-end application, a storytelling module to load a scenario, a module device-specific, a module for the upload of the scenario, a module for retrieving information from the REST API, and another module for the gamification features. An artificial intelligence module will be investigated in order to offer the possibility of suggest a possible scenario.

Features

The main features offered by the solution are as follows:

- A storytelling experience based that follows cinematography principles
- A script of each story that will depend on the used device (HTC Vive or HoloLens)
- The rendering of virtual characters and objects as component of the story
- The possibility to select a story (or scenario) from a menu in which a set of stories are available
- An appealing interface
- Gamification features: scores and achievements

CONCLUSION

This chapter has presented how the new technologies can be used to increase awareness in cyber security, including the description of a solution which combines extended reality and gamification to simulate scenarios involving virtual people and objects. This simulator can be potentially used to simulate a cyber attack as well as business training use cases. A possible improvement to this simulator could be the inclusion of artificial intelligence to propose a scenario to the user is also being heavily considered. For instance, the current version of the software only focuses on the manual activation of a pre-defined scenario. In the future, the automatic suggestion of a scenario would make the program more efficient in terms of goals achieving.

REFERENCES

Berglund, A., Gong, L., & Li, D. (2018). *Testing and validating Extended Reality (XR) technologies in manufacturing*. Academic Press.

Feiner, S., MaxIntyre, B., Höllerer, T., & Webster, A. (1997). A touring machine: Prototyping 3D mobile augmented reality systems for exploring the urban environment. Personal Technologies, 1(4), 208-217.

Feiner, S., MacIntyre, B., & Seligmann, D. (1993). Knowledge-based augmented reality. Communications of the ACM, 36(7), 53-62. doi:10.1145/159544.159587

Gironacci, I. M. (2019). Extended Reality Experiences Prediction using Collaborative Filtering. In SIGGRAPH Asia 2019 Doctoral Consortium (SA '19). Association for Computing Machinery. doi:10.1145/3366344.3366440

Hammerstein, J., & Mattson, J. (2017). *Cyber Affordance Visualization In Augmented Reality (CAVIAR)*. https://resources.sei.cmu.edu/asset_files/Presentation/2017_017_001_506490.pdf

Milgram, P., & Kishino, F. (1994). *A taxonomy of Mixed Reality visual displays*. Academic Press.

Munro, R. (2017). Immersive counter-terror training. *Crisis Response Journal, 13*(1), 84-85. http://www.target-h2020.eu/wp-content/uploads/2018/03/171031-CRJ-October-2017.pdf

Reicher, T., MacWilliams, A., & Brügges, B. (2004). *Study on Software Architectures for Augmented Reality systems*. Report to the ARVIKA consortium.

Research and Markets. (2018). *Global Mixed Reality Market – Growth, Trend and Forecasts (2018 – 2023)*. Retrieved from *Research and Markets* website: https://www.researchandmarkets.com/research/bfc4t3/global_mixed?w=4

Salazar, M., Gaviria, J., Laorden, C., & Bringas, P. G. (2013) Enhancing cybersecurity learning through an augmented reality-based serious game. *2013 IEEE Global Engineering Education Conference (EDUCON)*, 602–607. 10.1109/EduCon.2013.6530167

Sutherland, I. E. (1968). A head-mounted three-dimensional display. *Fall Joint Computer Conference, American Federation of Information Processing Societies.*

KEY TERMS AND DEFINITIONS

Augmented Reality: The AR (augmented reality) technology is relatively recent and constantly evolving. It is the representation of an altered reality in which, to the normal reality perceived by our senses, artificial and virtual information is superimposed, that is a series of information to be superimposed on what the eyes see.

Mixed Reality: Mixed reality is any technology that combines real elements with virtual elements. This classification follows the famous "reality-virtuality continuum" theorized at the same time by Milgram and Kishino, which shows that there is a spectrum of technologies that goes from pure real reality to pure virtual reality.

Virtual Reality: The VR (virtual reality) is a realistic simulation of a reality that does not exist. It comes from the combination of hardware and software devices that "collaborate" to create a virtual space within which the user can move freely. Access to this digital world is made possible by VR viewers and accessories (not just joypads, but also gloves, shoes and more) developed specifically to interact and "live" within virtual reality. In this way a simulated and three-dimensional world is created which in the eyes (but not only) of the users appears to be real.

About the Authors

Luisa Dall'Acqua is a senior cognitive scientist. She is an author, reviewer, and editor for several international scientific journals and book editions, and was a committee member for international Workshops/Conferences. Since 1990 she performed teaching activities, training students, teachers in service, headmasters and professionals; and since 2003 she was a member of international projects and research teams (USA, Europe, Asia). After an MSc in Philosophy, Luisa received a Ph.D. in Sociology of Legal Institutions and Policies, and a second Ph.D. in Psychological and Social Sciences. The main field of research is an engineering and social-cognitive approach to the intelligence and problem solving, and in particular to the decision-making risk under stress, conflict, and unpredictability, ranging from individual, collective, institutional intelligence applications to computational intelligence. The new risk scenarios, which she is working on, are Cyber-criminal profiling and Cyber-Intelligence in safety and security sectors of analysis. Furthermore, she is an expert Instructional Technologist and a digital communication professional. Currently, she is a permanent teacher at the TCO Scientific Lyceum (Italy) and an adjunct professor at the University of Bologna.

Irene M. Gironacci is currently working as Project Manager on Extended Reality research projects at the Swinburne University of Technology, and studying for a Ph.D. in Extended Reality and Artificial Intelligence. Previously, she has been working as a Mixed Reality Engineer on an H2020 project for training Security Agents at Luxembourg Institute of Science and Technology, Luxembourg, She has further experience as Scrum Master and R&D Consultant. Her research focuses on the following topics: new technologies, project management, risk management, artificial intelligence, 3D graphics, motion capture. She received both MSc and BSc in Software Engineering at University of Parma.

Index

6 Thinking Hats Method 57, 60

A

Augmented Reality 129, 142, 146-151, 153-159, 161-162, 166

C

Cognitive Biases 40-43, 49, 92, 96
Cognitive Science 60
cyber terrorism 123, 125, 134
Cyber Warfares 145

D

Decision-Making 1, 3, 18, 20-23, 25, 38, 40-41, 43, 46, 49-50, 56, 60, 64, 75-76, 89, 104, 118, 137

F

Foreign Policy 23, 25-26, 28, 38, 40-41, 43, 46-47, 53, 61-62, 103

G

Groupthink 40, 43, 45-47, 50-56, 60

H

HUMINT 106-107, 120, 122

I

Information Warfare 123, 138, 141, 145
Intelligence Analysis 11, 13-15, 53, 78-79, 92, 96, 104, 106, 122
Intelligence Analyst 1, 13, 15, 22, 39
Intelligence Collection 17, 106, 120, 122, 136
Intelligence Cycle 1, 15, 18, 20, 22, 122
Intelligence Organizations 106
Intelligence Politicization 104
internet of things 124, 129-130

L

Leadership Analysis 77-78
Leadership mindset 64

M

Micro Risk 91
Mixed Reality 129, 146-147, 149, 160-162, 166

O

OSINT 116-118, 120, 122

P

Policy research 3
Political Risk 80, 90-91
Polythink 40, 46-47, 52-56, 60
Problem Solving 6, 39

R

Reliability 17, 95
Risk Analysis 79, 82, 91, 128

S

Security policy 23

T

TECHINT 106, 115, 120, 122

U

Uncertainty 2, 10, 23, 25, 65, 79, 89

V

Virtual Reality 142, 146-148, 150, 156, 160-161, 166

Ensure Quality Research is Introduced to the Academic Community

Become an IGI Global Reviewer for Authored Book Projects

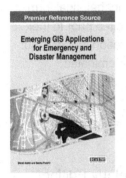
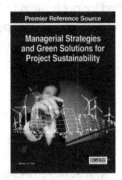

The overall success of an authored book project is dependent on quality and timely reviews.

In this competitive age of scholarly publishing, constructive and timely feedback significantly expedites the turnaround time of manuscripts from submission to acceptance, allowing the publication and discovery of forward-thinking research at a much more expeditious rate. Several IGI Global authored book projects are currently seeking highly-qualified experts in the field to fill vacancies on their respective editorial review boards:

Applications and Inquiries may be sent to:
development@igi-global.com

Applicants must have a doctorate (or an equivalent degree) as well as publishing and reviewing experience. Reviewers are asked to complete the open-ended evaluation questions with as much detail as possible in a timely, collegial, and constructive manner. All reviewers' tenures run for one-year terms on the editorial review boards and are expected to complete at least three reviews per term. Upon successful completion of this term, reviewers can be considered for an additional term.

If you have a colleague that may be interested in this opportunity, we encourage you to share this information with them.

IGI Global Proudly Partners With eContent Pro International

Receive a 25% Discount on all Editorial Services

Editorial Services

IGI Global expects all final manuscripts submitted for publication to be in their final form. This means they must be reviewed, revised, and professionally copy edited prior to their final submission. Not only does this support with accelerating the publication process, but it also ensures that the highest quality scholarly work can be disseminated.

English Language Copy Editing

Let eContent Pro International's expert copy editors perform edits on your manuscript to resolve spelling, punctuaion, grammar, syntax, flow, formatting issues and more.

Scientific and Scholarly Editing

Allow colleagues in your research area to examine the content of your manuscript and provide you with valuable feedback and suggestions before submission.

Figure, Table, Chart & Equation Conversions

Do you have poor quality figures? Do you need visual elements in your manuscript created or converted? A design expert can help!

Translation

Need your documjent translated into English? eContent Pro International's expert translators are fluent in English and more than 40 different languages.

Hear What Your Colleagues are Saying About Editorial Services Supported by IGI Global

"The service was very fast, very thorough, and very helpful in ensuring our chapter meets the criteria and requirements of the book's editors. I was quite impressed and happy with your service."

– Prof. Tom Brinthaupt,
Middle Tennessee State University, USA

"I found the work actually spectacular. The editing, formatting, and other checks were very thorough. The turnaround time was great as well. I will definitely use eContent Pro in the future."

– Nickanor Amwata, Lecturer,
University of Kurdistan Hawler, Iraq

"I was impressed that it was done timely, and wherever the content was not clear for the reader, the paper was improved with better readability for the audience."

– Prof. James Chilembwe,
Mzuzu University, Malawi

Email: customerservice@@econtentpro.com   www.igi-global.com/editorial-service-partners